THE UN**FOLD**ING
DRAMA
OF THE **BIBLE**

THE UN**FOLD**ING
DRA**MA**
OF THE **BIBLE**

Fourth Edition

Bernhard W.
ANDERSON

FORTRESS PRESS
Minneapolis

To the **L.Q.L.**
(Life Questers' League)

Contents

Preface to the Fourth Edition   7

Introducing the Bible Study   9

Study I: **Prologue: In the Beginning**   18

Study II: **A Way into the Future**   28

Study III: **The Discipline of Disaster**   39

Study IV: **A New Exodus**   47

Study V: **The People of the Torah**   56

Study VI: **Victory through Defeat**   66

Study VII: **The Church in the World**   74

Study VIII: **Epilogue: In the End**   81

Suggestions for Bible Study Leaders   91

Reading the Bible in the Twenty-First Century   99

Notes   107

About the Author   115

Preface to the Fourth Edition

This guide, which aims to help the reader understand the full sweep of the Bible from beginning to end, was originally prepared for the 1952 Religion in Life program at Bucknell University, sponsored by the Christian Association. To the surprise of many, including the author, it proved to have a wide appeal, far beyond the circle for whom it was originally intended. The guide was issued in revised form as a Haddam House Book in 1953 (later reprinted with only slight changes as a Reflection Book in 1957), followed by a second edition in 1971 that incorporated revisions based on almost two decades of use. A third edition was published by Fortress Press in 1988.

For this fourth edition, as in previous new editions, my policy has been to retain the basic outline and the original text as much as possible. In keeping with the times, however, I have added some new material:

- Responding to the interest in eschatology, or "the last things," I have included a final study section on 1 Thessalonians 4:13-18 called "The Triumphant Return."
- I have revised and expanded the postscript to the third edition ("The Dramatic Movement of Scripture") under the new title, "Reading the Bible in the Twenty-First Century." Here I talk about various perspectives on reading the Bible in the new millennium and about the approach of this book to the "unfolding drama" of Scripture.

Perceptive readers will note the introduction of the date abbreviations BCE (Before the Common Era) and CE (Common Era)—now widely accepted in literature that deals with the historical periods of the Old and New Testaments. As before, current standards of inclusive language are followed, and the "Suggestions for Bible Study Leaders" have been updated to take into account ongoing scholarly research.

The value of this book has been enhanced by several important contributions. Above all, I am grateful to my daughter, Carol Anderson Hanawalt, for her sensitive insights and her devoted assistance in editing the work and managing its publication. I would also like to thank my colleague and godchild, Judith H. Newman, for reviewing the bibliographic references and making valuable suggestions and additions, and my former student and colleague Steven Bishop, for his helpful review of the text.

The survival of this book through the decades is a clear indication that the study of the Bible is not a passing fad but remains a vital source of understanding for the community of faith and an irresistible challenge to many who seek a faith that is adequate to our times. Especially meaningful to me has been my lifelong association with a group of college friends known as the L.Q.L., or Life Questers' League. Starting as students at the College of the Pacific in California, members of this group have kept in touch with one another through the hastening years and have enjoyed each other's company in annual retreats for study, fellowship, and worship. To this extraordinary group I continue to dedicate this work, with the hope that others will find the study of the Bible helpful in the quest for a more abundant life.

Introducing the Bible Study

In one of his well-known sonnets, John Keats tells how in reading Chapman's translation of Homer he experienced the elation of a new discovery:

> Then felt I like some watcher of the skies
> When a new planet swims into his ken;
> Or, like stout Cortez, when with eagle eyes
> He stared at the Pacific—and all his men
> Looked at each other with a wild surmise—
> Silent, upon a peak in Darien.

In our time, many have had a similar experience in encountering the Bible. Bible study, of the kind you are about to engage in, can have the result of opening your eyes to a startling new vista, of giving you a new perspective upon the meaning of your life and your place in the whole historical drama.

There are two ways to approach the study of the Bible. The first is appropriate to classroom or academic study. Using this approach, one *looks at* the Bible from the outside as a spectator. One learns many interesting things about the Bible, such as the literary process that brought it to its final shape as a canon of sacred Scripture or the cultural, archaeological, and historical background of the various books. One is curious about the ideas of the Bible, even the "idea of God," and perhaps masters these ideas well enough to pass the course with flying colors. This descriptive approach has its place, but it is not the one we shall follow in these studies.

The second approach is one in which together we shall attempt to *stand within* the Bible and to look out at the world through the window of biblical faith. Like actors who put themselves into the script of a play, we shall read the Bible with personal involvement, realizing that it is not a textbook but a "letter from God with your personal address on it," as Søren Kierkegaard once put it. We shall read it as a story that is not just about other people of long ago but that is about us in the places where we are living. The language of the Bible, when it is truly heard, can be an event, a happening, such as it was with biblical witnesses, like Moses, who first were addressed personally by the God of Abraham, Isaac, and Jacob (Exod 3:4-6).

GOD'S MANIFESTO

The distinctiveness of this Bible study, which emphasizes the reader's identification with the plot of the story, arises from the uniqueness of the Bible itself. It is the Christian claim that the perspective set forth in the Bible has been provided by God's own self-revelation. This is what puts the Bible in a class by itself. The Bible is written not in a secret code, but in living human language that reveals the dramatic involvement of God in our personal lives and in our history. Christians affirm that the Bible contains the Word of God. Just as in our everyday experience, when a "word" is an event of communication between persons, so God's Word is an event of communication, an act of participation in the reality of our history (as we read in John 1:14, "The Word became flesh and dwelt among us"). This dynamic power of God's Word is a far cry from the notion that the Bible contains the literal, static words of God taken down by human stenographers. The Bible is not divine dictation, but divine drama whose language poetically exposes the meaning of human life in relation to the God who has condescended to dwell among us, in our human language and history. The Bible is, to use a familiar Christian formulation, the "Word of God in human words." This conviction underlies the practice in many churches of prefacing or concluding the reading of a Scripture selection with the phrase "The Word of God."

The Bible may be described as God's Manifesto. The dictionary defines a manifesto as "a public declaration, usually of a sovereign or political group, showing intentions and motives." So, for instance, the revolutionary *Communist Manifesto* of the nineteenth century defines economic struggle in terms of a predetermined movement of the historical process toward fulfillment in a classless society. Even today, to be a Communist is to understand one's existence in this context.

In a more special sense, the Bible is, for the Christian community, God's Manifesto. God is the Sovereign who declares the inner meaning of a historical crisis and discloses the direction of the whole human drama. God's revelation is given in the events of which the Bible is the record and the witness, events that come to climax and fulfillment in Jesus Christ. And to be a Christian is to understand one's existence in this dramatic context.

Now, this does not mean one must be a convinced Christian before anything can be gotten out of the study of the Bible. As Paul Lehmann once observed, "The Bible has a curious slant in favor of the unbeliever; the unbeliever, that is, who is really honest about his unbelief, and really curious about the full diversity and complexity of the world in which he lives."[1] → sounds like me ☺

The only condition for fruitful Bible study is that you come with an open mind and an unbounded interest in the question, "What is the meaning of my life and the historical crisis in which I and my community are involved?" This means:

- You must be willing to let the past—this biblical past—speak to you where you are living, to make a claim upon you in the present.
- You must meet others in the group as persons, respecting their individuality and being willing to learn from the conversation.

- You must come with the intention of wrestling seriously
  and honestly with the meaning of a biblical passage—not
  to air your private opinions or prejudices.
- You must be ready to hear what the great teachers of the
  church have had to say in their commentaries—Augustine,
  Calvin, Luther, and others, including those of our own
  period.
- You must expect to be questioned by the Bible, even as
  you bring your own questions to the Bible.

It may be that in this give-and-take experience you will discover
an entirely new dimension of life, as you find yourself drawn into
the history that God is making.

THE BIBLE AS A WHOLE

In this book we shall tackle the whole Bible. This may seem as
foolish as American tourists who breeze through the Louvre as
though they are trying to establish a new track record. It is admit-
ted at the outset that this approach runs the risk of superficiality.
It is hoped that you will have time enough to stake your claims
so that later you can come back to sink your shafts more deeply,
aided perhaps by the "Suggestions for Further Reading" given at
the end of each study unit.

Many people, however, lack any awareness of the Bible as a
whole. They know a few snatches of Scripture here and there, like
the twenty-third Psalm or the Sermon on the Mount, but are very
hazy—if not completely ignorant—about the larger dramatic
context within which these favorite passages have meaning. We all
need to stand back from the trees so that we may see the woods.
That is the justification for this study of the Bible in eight units.

In the following pages we shall consider the Bible as presenting
a historical drama.[2] To be sure, this figure of speech is not found
anywhere in the Bible itself, but it is a convenient and appropriate
way to view the Bible as a whole. Several characteristics of a drama

immediately spring to mind. For one thing, a drama has a beginning and an end—it starts somewhere and goes somewhere. Also, it has a cast of persons, and the story deals with the whole range of human experience, from triumph to tragedy. Furthermore, a drama has a plot that moves forward through several acts toward a denouement (or climax) in which the episodes that took place at the beginning are understood in their larger meaning. In a drama there is a great deal of diversity: different personalities, different attitudes toward life, different episodes that take place at different times and in various settings. But underlying all this variety is the movement of the plot toward its resolution.

The Bible, too, has a unity like that of a great drama. It moves from beginning to end, from creation to new creation. The story deals with people's hopes and fears, their joy and anguish, their ambitions and failures. There is a great deal of diversity in the Bible: different authors, different historical situations, different kinds of theological expression. But underlying all this great variety is the dynamic movement, similar to the plot of a drama, that binds the whole together.

The biblical drama, however, is unique in that God appears in the cast. Not only is God the Author who stands behind the scenes prompting and directing the drama, but God also enters onto the stage of history as the Chief Actor—the protagonist. The biblical plot is the working out of God's purpose for the creation in spite of all efforts to oppose it. The denouement is reached, according to the conviction of the Christian community, when the crucifixion and resurrection of Jesus of Nazareth are proclaimed as the sign of God's decisive victory. In the light of this climactic event, the earlier stages of the story are understood with a deeper and larger meaning.

A DRAMA IN THREE ACTS

Our series of eight studies will follow this dramatic scheme:

Prologue	STUDY I: In the Beginning
ACT I	THE FORMATION OF GOD'S PEOPLE
Scene 1	STUDY II: A Way into the Future
Scene 2	STUDY III: The Discipline of Disaster
ACT II	THE RE-FORMATION OF GOD'S PEOPLE
Scene 1	STUDY IV: The New Exodus
Scene 2	STUDY V: The People of the Torah
ACT III	THE TRANSFORMATION OF GOD'S PEOPLE
Scene 1	STUDY VI: Victory through Defeat
Scene 2	STUDY VII: The Church in the World
Epilogue	STUDY VIII: In the End

It ought to become clear that each of the acts in the dramatic scheme interprets a decisive historical event that is proclaimed as a "mighty act" of God. The three crucial moments in the biblical drama are:

1. The exodus of oppressed Israelites from Egypt and the opening of a way into the future out of a no-exit situation;
2. The exile of conquered Israelites into Babylonia and their miraculous liberation for a new beginning in their homeland;
3. The crucifixion and resurrection of Jesus, which reconstituted the people of God as God's task force in the world.

The selection of passages for the study of these three major "acts" of God has to be somewhat arbitrary, for obviously we can deal with only a small fraction of the relevant biblical material.[3] Our purpose is not to make an exhaustive study of the Bible but to enter into the meaning of these three crucial stages of the biblical drama.

GETTING INTO THE ACT

One final word: Do not suppose that this is the kind of drama one can view from a grandstand seat. We are not to be spectators of something that happened once upon a time. The Bible is not a book of ancient history. It is more like the commedia dell'arte, a dramatic form that flourished in sixteenth-century Italy.[4] In this kind of drama, the players were asked to improvise, to put themselves into the story. To be sure, it was not a free improvisation, for there were some given elements: there was the director, there was a company of actors, and there was a story plot that was given to them in broad outline. With these given elements they were told to improvise—that is, to fill in the gaps on their own.

In this Bible study we are called upon to improvise—that is, to put ourselves into the story and to fill in the gaps with our own experience. We must be ready to get onto the biblical stage and participate personally—along with the "company," the community of faith—in the dramatic movement of the plot, act by act. Perhaps this warning is unnecessary, for it is the testimony of many generations that when the Bible is read in the community of faith the Holy Spirit enhances the human words of Scripture with new meaning and power. As a result, people become actors in what Amos Wilder calls "the great story and plot of all time and space" and are drawn into relation with God, the Great Dramatist.[5]

Thus, realizing that the Great Dramatist is apt to lure us from the spectator's balcony and put us into the act, we begin our study.

Suggestions for Further Reading

Anderson, Bernhard W. "The Contemporaneity of the Bible." *Princeton Seminary Bulletin* 62 (1969): 38–50.

———. *The Living Word of the Bible*. Philadelphia: Westminster, 1979.

————. *Understanding the Old Testament*. 5th ed. (with S. Bishop and J. Newman). Upper Saddle River, N.J.: Pearson Prentice Hall, 2006. See the Introduction, especially "The Story of the Bible." The 5th edition is cited throughout this book.

Brown, Robert McAffee. *The Bible Speaks to You*. Philadelphia: Westminster, 1955.

Fackre, Gabriel. *A Narrative Interpretation of Basic Christian Doctrine*, vol. 1, and *Authority: Scripture in the Church for the World Today*, vol. 2 of *The Christian Story*. Grand Rapids, Mich.: Eerdmans, 1978–87. A Christian theologian maintains that doctrine gives expression to the story that unfolds in the Bible and gives it authority.

Gomes, Peter J. *The Good Book: Reading the Bible with Mind and Heart*. New York: William Morrow, 1996.

Herberg, Will. "Biblical Faith as *Heilsgeschichte*: The Meaning of Redemptive History in Human Existence." In *Faith Enacted as History: Essays in Biblical Theology*. Edited by B. W. Anderson. Philadelphia: Westminster Press, 1976.

Holladay, William L. *Long Ago God Spoke: How Christians May Hear the Old Testament Today*. Philadelphia: Augsburg Fortress Press, 1995. Addresses problems modern Christians find in appropriating the Old Testament as sacred scripture.

Niebuhr, H. Richard. *The Meaning of Revelation*. New York: Macmillan, 1941. See chapter 2, "The Story of Our Life."

Sanders, James A. *Torah and Canon*. Philadelphia: Fortress Press, 1972.

Schneiders, Sandra. *The Revelatory Text: Interpreting the New Testament as Sacred Scripture*. San Francisco: HarperSanFrancisco, 1992.

Commentaries and Other Study Aids

HarperCollins Bible Dictionary. Edited by Paul J. Achtemeier. Rev. and updated ed. San Francisco: HarperSanFrancisco, 1996. Excellent maps and commentary.

HarperCollins Study Bible: New Revised Standard Version with the Apocryphal/Deuterocanonical Books. Edited by Wayne Meeks. San Francisco: HarperSanFrancisco, 1997. Compiled under the direction of the Society of Biblical Literature, with generous annotations and particular attention to historical context.

New English Bible with the Apocrypha: Oxford Study Edition. Edited by Samuel Sandmel. New York: Oxford University Press, 1976.

New Interpreter's Study Bible. Edited by Walter J. Harrelson. Nashville, Tenn.: Abingdon, 2003. An edition of the New Revised Standard Version of the Bible, with commentary and notes by an ecumenical team of scholars.

New Jerome Bible Commentary. Edited by Raymond E. Brown, J. A. Fitzmyer, and Roland E. Murphy. Englewood Cliffs, N.J.: Prentice Hall, 1990. A fine commentary by Roman Catholic scholars.

New Oxford Annotated Bible: NRSV with the Apocrypha. 3rd ed. Edited by Michael D. Coogan. New York: Oxford University Press, 2001.

Oxford Bible Commentary. Edited by John Barton and John Muddiman. New York: Oxford University Press, 2001.

Prologue:
In the **Beginning**

Study Passages

1. Genesis 1:1—2:3
   The Creation of the Universe
2. Psalm 8
   The Human Role in God's Creation
3. Psalm 104
   The Wonderful Order of Creation
4. Genesis 2:4b—3:24
   Paradise Lost

One of the daringly original themes of the biblical drama is expressed in the majestic announcement found in the first words of Genesis: "In the beginning God created the heavens and the earth." We are so used to speaking of God as Creator that we scarcely realize the revolutionary implications of this belief. According to the religions of ancient Egypt and Babylonia, the gods were in nature, for nature with its creative powers (symbolized, for instance, by the sun and moon) was regarded as a manifestation of the divine. In Babylonia, creation was seen to be caught up in a natural process that moves in a great circle toward the new creation at the turn of the year, the time of the New Year's festival.

Likewise, for the ancient Greeks, the gods were immanent, or "inside" nature, and since the cosmos was regarded as eternal, there was no place in their thought for creation. The Bible stands in flat contradiction to these views. God is not immanent in nature; God is not a natural process. Rather, God is "over against" nature or, to use a philosophical term, is *transcendent*. Nature is not divine but displays the handiwork of its creator (Ps 19:1) in the same way a painting displays the artistry of the painter. Heaven and earth (that is, everything that is) are seen to be part of the majestic purpose of God, which moves in a vast sweep from beginning to end, from creation to consummation.[1]

LIFE'S DIMENSION OF DEPTH

A roadblock for our approach to Genesis 1–3 is our bondage to the scientific attitude. Too many people try to modernize these chapters into a scientific account and to harmonize the narrative with modern scientific theories. Some have argued, for instance, that the "days" mentioned in Genesis 1 correspond to geological periods, or that the doctrine of evolution is implicit in the whole account (note that the emergence of biological life is associated with the waters in 1:20-23). But this is to confuse biblical language, which is poetic and imaginative, with scientific language, which is descriptive and analytical.[2] The central issue here is that of the *ultimate meaning* of human life in the natural sphere, and this is not a scientific question, properly speaking. The Bible asks—and answers—the question about human existence (the so-called existential question): "What is the origin, meaning, and destiny of human life?" One must be on guard against reading into the biblical narrative the presuppositions of our scientific age. It would be advisable to read the creation account in Genesis 1 in the context of some psalms, especially Psalms 8 and 104. This is poetic language that intends to praise the God whose purpose enfolds all things and upon whom every creature, human and nonhuman, is radically dependent for existence (see Ps 104:27-30).[3]

It is now generally known that we have two creation stories in Genesis, the first running from Gen 1:1 to Gen 2:3, and the second beginning with the last half of Gen 2:4 (after a transitional editorial statement, "These are the generations of . . ."). The first of these accounts received its final literary formulation in the period of the Exile, the period we are symbolizing as

Act II (about 550 BCE), although it was probably used liturgically in temple services long before its final composition. The second account, on the other hand, comes from the period of Act I, perhaps as early as the era of Solomon (about 950 BCE), though it probably circulated in oral tradition long before this. Each story expresses the viewpoint of the theological circle in which it was composed, just as it reflects the language and culture of its period.[4] The important thing to notice, however, is that despite the differences in style and content, both accounts affirm that the ultimate meaning of human life is disclosed not in the processes of nature but in relationship to the God who transcends the whole realm of nature. God is the Author, Sustainer, and Finisher of all that is. These stories are really word pictures that portray life's deepest dimension.[5]

It would be helpful if in English we had words corresponding to the German words *Weltbild*, "world picture," and *Weltanschauung*, "world perspective." The world picture of Genesis 1 is the naive one of antiquity—a picture of the earth as a flat surface, resting on the primeval "waters beneath the earth" and separated from the "waters above the earth" by a blue firmament (Gen 2:6-7). Were it not for the Creator's sustaining power, the waters would return to their original place and engulf the world in chaos, as almost happened once upon a time, according to the Flood story (Gen 6:5—9:17; see especially 7:11-24).

The world perspective, however, concerns the meaning of the human drama enacted on the stage of nature and in relation to the natural environment. Notice that humans and animals are created on the same day (Gen 1:24-28)—a fine poetic indication of humanity's involvement in, and dependence upon, the world of nature. But human beings are not just animals who live in, and adjust to, their natural environment. They are able to survey and control nature, to search for the good, the true, and the beautiful, to remember the past, to hope for the future, and to decide in the present. Elevated to a royal position "a little lower than God," as a Hebrew poet exclaimed, they are given dominion over God's earthly estate (Ps 8:5-8). The same view is expressed

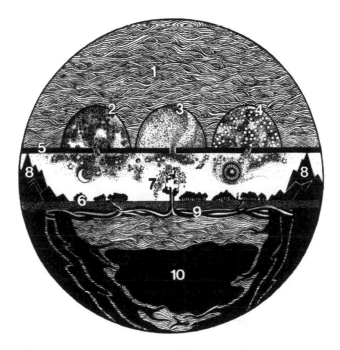

The Ancient Pictorial View of the Universe

1. The waters above (and below) the earth
2–4. Chambers of hail, rain, snow
5. The firmament with its "sluices"
6. The surface of the earth
7. The navel of the earth: "fountain of the great deep"
8. The mountain pillars supporting the firmament
9. Sweet waters (rivers, lakes, seas) on which the earth floats
10. Sheol, the realm of death (the "pit")

in Gen 1:26-28, where at the climax of God's creation 'adam
(an inclusive Hebrew word meaning "human being," "humankind") is made "in the image of God." 'Adam consists of equal
partners, "male and female," who are to "image" or represent
God on earth by ruling wisely and benevolently over the nonhuman creation.[6]

The story in Genesis 2 is written from a similar point of view.
Like the animals, the human being ('adam) is made from the
dust and returns to the dust (2:7; 3:19), but this creature's ability
to name the animals indicates human superiority and dominion
(2:19-20). Today we know about the chemical constituents of
this dust, and we have a completely different cosmology or world
picture corresponding to the dimensions of our Space Age. But
have we gone beyond the biblical perspective on the meaning of
human life in relation to its natural environment?

This question perhaps gains in significance when we turn
from biology to other fields of human endeavor, such as art,
philosophy, and history. For example, the historian Herbert
Butterfield, once a professor of modern history at the University
of Cambridge, observed that the historian does not treat humanity "as essentially a part of nature or consider [it] primarily in
this aspect," as the biologist usually does. Rather, the historian
"picks up the other end of the stick and envisages a world of
human relations standing, so to speak, over against nature," and
this leads to a study of the "new kind of life" that human beings
have "superimposed on the jungle, the forest and the waste."
He goes on to say: "Since this world of human relations is the
historian's universe, we may say that history is a human drama
of personalities, taking place as it were on the stage of nature,
and amid its imposing scenery."[7]

Thus we speak of the human drama, although often in purely
humanistic terms. The creation story underscores the conviction
that the drama is not just about human beings; rather, it is a
"cosmic journey" that has its beginning and end in the purpose
of God. Hence the whole drama is enacted within the horizons
of "In the beginning God . . ." and "In the end God . . ."

PARADISE LOST

Much attention can be devoted to the narrative of paradise lost in Genesis 2 and 3, for here are to be found the most profound insights into the human situation. Don't be disturbed by the picturesque and naive narrative style, as though this marked the story as inferior to the elevated prose of Genesis 1. Notice that the story has all the features of a good story: It has a beginning and an end, a cast of characters who act in relation to one another, and a plot that dynamically moves toward a denouement or resolution. And most interesting, God, the Creator, appears as the main Actor in the story and enters into personal relationship with the man and the woman, even asking searching questions: "Where are you?" "Who told you that you were naked?" "What is this that you have done?" Reflect on the meaning of some of the symbols in the story: "one flesh," "the subtle serpent," "the tree of life," "the tree of knowledge of good and evil," nakedness, banishment from the garden, and so forth.

This is not just a story of something that happened once upon a time but is a profound description of the human situation in any historical time. The human actors—the first man and woman—represent everybody. Surely there is in human experience a melancholy awareness that life is not what it ought to be, that somehow or somewhere human beings have lost the "peace" (wholeness, well-being) and the humanness that the Creator intended. Conflict, anxiety, insecurity, exploitation, injustice, suffering, guilt—these are not intended to be normal, even though they are life's daily realities. Why is this? Unlike Marxism, which traces the problem to economic factors, and unlike Oriental religions (Hinduism, Buddhism), which advocate liberation from the illusory realm of sensory desire, the Bible traces the problem to something in human nature: to the human will, to human freedom. The temptation to be independent or even to be "like God" (3:5)—that is, to live life in our own way and on our own terms—leads to estrangement at all levels: from God, from others, and from the earth itself.

Notice that the paradise story falls into three episodes:

1. In the first episode, the narrator portrays peace in God's beautiful garden ("paradise" is an old Persian word meaning an "enclosed park"). The human being has a God-given task: to care for ("dress and keep") God's garden. Work, when performed with responsibility and dignity, is intended to be creative and fulfilling. Above all, the human being is enjoined to take care of God's garden, not to violate and pollute nature. The God-given task, however, cannot be performed alone; in fact, to quote a German proverb, *Ein Mensch ist kein Mensch* ("One human being is no human being at all"). So the narrator portrays the moving scene of God's creation of a woman so that the two companions may stand vis-à-vis, face-to-face, and even be joined in the most intimate relationship as "one flesh." The story of God's creation is not complete until *'adam* is differentiated into "the man" and "the woman," the two beings who correspond to each other and who are equally responsible in caring for God's estate.[8]

2. In the second episode, the narrator portrays rebellion in the garden. The freedom that God has given the human companions places them in a situation of decision. Why be content with creaturely limitations? Why not reach out for forbidden fruit? The "theological" argument of the serpent is subtle and seductive, and the couple cannot resist the tempting possibilities of life on their own terms. The meaning of the phrase "knowing good and evil" is not altogether clear, but it seems to be a Hebrew expression for the mature and even divine wisdom required for making difficult decisions (see 2 Sam 14:17; 1 Kgs 3:9). Sin, then, is the presumption that human beings can grasp such wide and penetrating knowledge that they can live on their own resources, without dependence upon God. Sin is a declaration of independence from God; it is the refusal to "let God be God." Above all, it should be understood that sin is not just a matter of doing something immoral, of being "bad." Sin is, in a profound sense, a false maturity, illustrated in Jesus' parable

of the prodigal son who independently goes off into a far country and wastes his substance in a life of abandon (Luke 15:11-24). The consequence, according to the paradise story, is alienation from God, from other human beings, and from one's truest self—an alienation that is rooted in a rebellious will that oversteps creaturely boundaries.

3. In the third episode (3:8–24), the narrator portrays judgment in the garden. "The love story," to use Phyllis Trible's apt words, has "gone awry." Now that the nakedness of the man and woman has been exposed, they are described as fugitives running to hide behind the trees of the garden from God, who strolls in the garden in the cool of the day. Notice the severe consequences of misused creaturely freedom. Judgment falls first upon the serpent, who proved to be more than simply an animal of the field but became a symbol of the sinister power of evil. The next consequence was that the relation between the sexes was impaired: henceforth childbirth would be painful for the woman and she would be in a subordinate relationship to her husband. The final consequence was that the man's work would become tedious and he would have to fight to eke out a livelihood from the soil.

The story of paradise lost ends with the picture of the two human beings, representatives of the human race, cast out from the primeval peace of the garden into a restless historical life of insecurity and conflict. The rest of the Bible, beginning with the tragic sequence of stories portrayed in Genesis 4–11 (Cain's murder of Abel, Lamech's blood revenge, violence leading to the Flood, the Tower of Babel), bears witness to the religious truth that when human beings misuse their God-given freedom, they are estranged from God, from others, and from their deepest selves. For humans belong to God by nature and cannot find peace outside the relationship for which they were created. So Augustine began his *Confessions* with this prayer: "O Lord, thou hast made us for thyself, and our hearts are restless until they rest in thee."

Questions to Think About

1. Discuss the difference between the "truth" of the biblical account of creation and the "truth" that we usually regard as scientific. What did it mean for astronauts to broadcast the opening verses of Genesis as their Christmas 1968 message from the moon?

2. In a famous essay, "The Historical Roots of Our Ecologic Crisis" (*Science* 155 [1967]: 1203–7; reprinted in various contexts), Lynn White Jr. maintained that the Jewish-Christian faith is largely responsible for the present "rape of nature," because in Gen 1:26-28 human beings are commissioned to have dominion over nature. Discuss this thesis in the light of the announcement in Genesis 1 that human beings are made in the "image" of God, or the portrayal in Genesis 2 of the human being as the caretaker of the garden.

3. With the story of Genesis 2–3 before you, paraphrase the meaning of "sin" (noting that the word "sin" does not appear in that story). Can sin find expression in moral goodness as well as in immoral acts? What light, if any, does Albert Camus's novel *The Fall* throw on the story?

4. Discuss the equality of man and woman in the light of the "image of God" passage in Genesis 1 and the portrayal of man and woman as companions in the story in Genesis 2. Do you understand the story to mean that the subordination of woman was not part of God's creation but was a consequence of "the fall"?

5. A British writer, James Bryce, once observed that the American Constitution, with its system of checks and balances upon the exercise of power, was written by men who believed in "original sin." Is this realistic? Compare the Marxist view that the troubles of history are traceable to economic factors, and that when these are changed human nature will be transformed. (George Orwell's *Animal Farm* may give some food for thought.)

6. Compare the picture of creation presented in Genesis 1 with that of Psalm 104. Why is the story in Genesis 2–3 (paradise lost) a necessary supplement to the view of the human role in God's creation as set forth in Genesis 1?

Suggestions for Further Reading

Anderson, Bernhard W. *Contours of Old Testament Theology.* Minneapolis: Fortress Press, 1999. See especially chapter 11, "Creation and the Noachic Covenant."

———. "Creation and Ecology." In *Creation in the Old Testament.* Edited by B. W. Anderson. Philadelphia: Fortress Press, 1984. See especially pp. 152–69.

———. *Creation versus Chaos.* Eugene, Ore.: Wipf and Stock, 2005; orig. publ. Philadelphia: Fortress Press, 1967/1987.

———. *Understanding the Old Testament.* 5th ed. (with S. Bishop and J. Newman). Upper Saddle River, N.J.: Pearson Prentice Hall, 2006.

Brueggemann, Walter. *Genesis.* Atlanta: John Knox, 1982. See especially pp. 23–54. Highly recommended.

Joranson, Philip N., and Ken Butigan, eds. *Cry of the Environment: Rebuilding the Christian Creation Tradition.* Santa Fe, N.Mex.: Bear, 1984.

Rad, Gerhard von. *Genesis.* Old Testament Library. Philadelphia: Westminster Press, 1961; rev. ed., 1972. One of the best commentaries on Genesis.

Sarna, Nahum. *Understanding Genesis.* New York: McGraw-Hill, 1966; New York: Schocken Books, 1970. A clear and illuminating exposition by a Jewish scholar.

Trible, Phyllis. "The Topical Clue" and "A Love Story Gone Awry." In *God and the Rhetoric of Sexuality.* Philadelphia: Fortress Press, 1978. An exquisite and insightful interpretation.

A **Way** into the **Future**

Study Passages

1. Exodus 3:1-21
   The Call of Moses
2. Exodus 19:3-6; 20:1-17
   Keeping the Covenant
3. Exodus 24:3-8
   Ceremony of Covenant Making
4. Deuteronomy 4:25-40; 5:1-53; 8:1-20
   Sermonic Interpretations of Exodus and Covenant

With the Exodus (the "going out") of the Israelites from Egypt, the curtain rises on the first major act of the biblical drama. Every historical community recalls some decisive event as its birth hour. Of this formative event the members of the community can say: "This is what brought us forth upon the stage of history as a people, with a shared tradition and a sense of destiny. This is where the meaning of our history was disclosed." In the United States, for instance, Americans celebrate the Revolutionary War and the signing of the Declaration of Independence as decisive events in the formation of the country. It is significant that in a grave crisis Abraham Lincoln harked back to that creative moment: "Fourscore and seven years ago our fathers brought forth on this continent a new nation, conceived in liberty."

ISRAEL'S BIRTH HOUR

It was similar in the case of the community known as Israel, to which the church is intimately related. Still, the analogy of

America and Israel breaks down for a couple of reasons. For one thing, the term *Israel,* as used in the Old Testament, cannot be equated with a nation. This will come as a surprise to many, because today Israel is the name of a powerful state in the Middle East, one of the members of the United Nations. But in the two centuries preceding David (about 1200–1000 BCE), before Israel became a monarchic state "like the nations" (compare 1 Sam 8:4-9), the term applied to a people loosely bound in a covenant federation. And the term continued to be used for the covenant people after the fall of the nation in 587 BCE. Thus Israel, in the first and last analysis, transcends political and ethnic categories. In this larger sense, Paul speaks of the community of faith, embracing both Jews and Gentiles, as the Israel of God (Gal 5:16).

Moreover, for the people Israel the Exodus was not just an ordinary event of history. Its meaning was revealed in a theological dimension as the event that gave them a special "calling" or vocation. The prophet Hosea used parental imagery to describe God's special relationship to this people:

> When Israel was a child, I loved him,
> and out of Egypt I called my son.
> (Hos 11:1)

And another prophet, Isaiah, described the Exodus as the time when God created Israel to be a people so that they might perform a task in the divine purpose (Isa 51:9-11).

It is significant that Israel's ancient confession of faith found expression in the retelling of a story in which the Exodus was the focal event. The confession ran something like this: "Our ancestors were pilgrims in Palestine, wandering from place to place. A small band went down to Egypt in a time of famine, and when Israel multiplied, the Egyptian king subjected *us* to slave labor on public works. But the God of our ancestors saw *our* affliction and heard *our* cry. With many marvelous signs of divine concern and care, God delivered *us* from Pharaoh's yoke and brought us into a new land where we could find our freedom in the service of God." In this paraphrase of Deut 26:5-9, note how the individual worshiper identifies with the story, as evidenced in the first person pronouns "our" and "us." Even today the Passover ceremony emphasizes the involvement of the observant Jew in that momentous event.

These crucial events, especially the central event of the Exodus, exerted a powerful influence upon the religious imagination of the people in the new situations in which they found themselves in their historical pilgrimage. The God whom Israel worships is the God who comes to a band of slaves in the time of oppression and opens a way into the future where there is no way. The imagery of the Israelite story has had a great appeal to Christians in many ages, as witnessed by the preaching of the Reverend Dr. Martin Luther King Jr., whose "dream" for America was infused with the imagery of liberation from Pharaoh's yoke and a march through the wilderness toward the promised land.[1]

The best way to prepare for this study is to read as much as possible of Exodus 1–24 and the later commentary on the meaning of these events found in Deuteronomy 1–11. Here our primary concern is not with critical details.[2] Rather, we want to enter into the inner meaning of the Exodus drama—the meaning that was kept alive and relived in every annual celebration of the Passover feast and in periodic covenant renewal services at the central sanctuary (Joshua 24). This can be done by concentrating on the passages that have been selected, perhaps with side reference to the sermonic material in Deut 4:25-40 or 8:1-20. It would be advisable to bypass the question of particular miracle stories for the time being (for example, the plagues) and to concentrate instead on the central miracle of "the mystery of Israel"—the elected people that has survived to this day.

ENCOUNTER WITH GOD

A good place to begin the discussion is with the story of Moses's call in Exodus 3, for this narrative presents the theme of the whole Book of Exodus. Rather than tripping over literal details, read the passage with religious imagination. Perhaps you will find that the dialogue sounds deep notes with which you resonate in your own experience. Notice that Moses was brought into an I-thou relation to God not as he was overwhelmed by the grandeur of nature, but as he was brooding over the meaning of a historical situation: the plight of his kinsfolk who were crying out under oppression in Egypt. The narrator emphasizes the theme of God's entrance into the human struggle: "I have seen the plight of my people"; "I have heard their cry"; "I know their sorrows"; "I have come down to rescue them." The God of the Exodus is not removed from the places where people are struggling and suffering; rather, God is involved, liberating people from bondage and opening a way into the future.

The story of Moses's encounter with God is paralleled in other accounts, like the portrayal of Elijah's contest on Mount Horeb (Sinai) (1 Kings 19), the call of a prophet (see Jer 1:4-19), a psalmist's awareness of the God who is inescapable (Psalm 139), and the symphony of voices in the New Testament that proclaim that God has spoken and acted in the life, death, and resurrection of Jesus Christ. Therefore, when we speak of revelation we are referring to a personal encounter in which the holy God, who is not a phenomenon of our human world, becomes manifest in the world through word and deed.

Perhaps a human analogy will help to clarify this. We cannot really know any person unless the person discloses herself or himself through speech and action. We can know a lot of things about the person, such as family background, education, job, physical appearance, and so on, but we cannot really know him or her in an I-thou relationship apart from self-disclosure in what the person says or does.[3] So it is with God. We cannot know God personally unless God chooses to speak through inspired words and to act with liberating power. Revelation is not receiving ideas about God through some private pipeline of communication; rather, it is God's act of self-disclosure, which results in a new understanding of who we are and of our task in the divine purpose. And this encounter takes place in the concrete situations of human history.

GOD'S PERSONAL NAME

One interesting motif of the Moses story is the giving of God's name. In the ancient world a personal name was not just a label, as it usually is for us, but was closely connected with the person of the bearer. One's name was believed to be a disclosure of one's identity and one's character. Moses, we are told, was reluctant to go back to Egypt because his kinsfolk would surely ask the name of the God who had commissioned him. Moses was given God's name, so the story goes, but only indirectly and evasively—for "I am who I am" is a wordplay on the personal name (Hebrew: *YHWH*) that the Israelites were to use in worship.[4]

The giving of God's name (that is, God's self) symbolizes God's self-giving, God's self-presentation, to a people. Those who know the name of God know who God is (God's personal identity) and can pray to God in the I-thou relationship of prayer. God is truly present in the midst of the people. But God's name cannot be "taken in vain," that is, used for human purposes, as in some societies even today in which the knowledge of a personal name gives magical power over the bearer. The holy God, who descends voluntarily to the level of the people and identifies with their struggle for liberation, is not subject to human control or manipulation. A close relationship to God does not entitle the people to say that God is "our God" in a possessive sense—the prisoner of their thoughts, social values, or national ambitions. God reserves the freedom to act in surprising ways: "I will be gracious to whom I will be gracious, and will show mercy on whom I will show mercy" (Exod 33:19). God keeps the initiative.

The prophets of Israel helped the people understand what it means to say, "God is with us" (Hebrew: *immanuel*; compare Isa 7:1-17). It means to seek good and not evil and to establish justice (Amos 5:14-15). It means to realize that God's saving action includes the "strange work" of divine judgment upon God's own people (Isa 28:21-22). It means to experience the "new thing" of God's grace and forgiveness, which makes possible a new beginning (Isa 43:16-21). The God whom Israel knows and worships is the God who does surprising things that demand a reconsideration of past beliefs, reevaluation of old standards, reinterpretation of previous tradition. And perhaps the greatest surprise of all comes with the New Testament announcement that Jesus of Nazareth is Immanuel, "God with us" (Matt 2:23). Indeed, according to the Gospel of John, his mission is to manifest God's "name" (nature) to the disciples (John 17:6).

THE COVENANT COMMITMENT

The next three passages (Exod 19:3-6; 20:1-17; 24:3-8) should be considered together, for they deal with Israel's response to God's intervention on its behalf. Here we come upon the central motif of the biblical drama: the Covenant (Old Testament really means "Old Covenant" and New Testament means "New Covenant"). As in the case of the marriage covenant, this biblical covenant is a personal relationship based on commitment and trust. Unlike the marriage covenant, however, it is more unilateral in character, for it is a covenant between unequals—God and people. It is God who "makes" or "gives" the covenant; Israel responds in gratitude, reverence, and loyalty.

Much light has been shed upon the nature of the Mosaic covenant from ancient treaties or covenants that governed the relationships between peoples during the period before David. Among the archives of the ancient Hittites (a people who ruled in Asia Minor, which is modern Turkey, from 1600 to 1200 BCE) archaeologists have found copies of treaties between the Hittite suzerain and the vassal states. The treaty form includes several major elements. To begin with, the "great king" announces his name and titles and declares the benevolent deeds he has performed on behalf of the vassal state. There follows a list of stipulations, including the prohibition of entering into foreign alliances, which are binding upon the vassal in gratitude for favors received. Then, for the vassal who takes the oath of loyalty, these legal stipulations are sanctioned by the invocation of blessing and curse—blessing for obedience, and curse (judgment) for betrayal of the covenant. The treaty form also includes a provision for periodic public reading of the covenant laws and the renewal of the vows of allegiance.[5]

In many respects the covenant between God and Israel is similar to this ancient covenant form, showing that Israel used a prevalent literary vehicle to confess its faith in the God who claimed this people in the event of the Exodus. Israel, however, put a new picture into the old frame. The following points deserve consideration:

1. God takes the initiative in establishing the covenant relationship. God enters into the historical situation in an act of self-giving (disclosure of the name) and in acts of benevolence toward a people in distress. Israel does not first choose but is *chosen*. Therefore, faith is wholehearted response to God's initiative as manifested in the "mighty act" that liberates a people from bondage and opens a way into the future.

2. This relationship puts people under an absolute demand: "Thou shalt," "Thou shalt not." In the Decalogue, God addresses the people with categorical imperatives, and they are responsible before God in all the relationships of life. One cannot serve God with half of one's heart and some other loyalty with the other half. Like any absolute commitment, the covenant allegiance is essentially a "jealous" one. In this connection, read the Shema ("Hear") found in Deut 6:4-5, which is the central creed of Judaism to this day.

3. The covenant involves not only obligations toward God but obligations toward the other members of the community. This is the meaning of the giving of the law in connection with the making of the covenant. The legal stipulations are adapted to new cultural circumstances,

but the basic principle remains constant: persons are absolutely responsible to one another because they are absolutely responsible to God.

4. Ethical responsibility is motivated by gratitude for *what God has done*—for the acts of benevolence manifested in the event of the Exodus. Notice the preface to the Ten Commandments: "I am the Lord [*Yahweh*] your God, who brought you out of the land of Egypt, out of the house of bondage." Israelites are to obey God not as slaves driven to their duties but as a liberated people who stand in awe and gratitude before the gracious deeds of their Redeemer.

5. The Mosaic covenant contains a conditional element: "*If* you will obey my voice and keep my covenant . . ." (Exod 19:3-6). Faithfulness to the covenant yields blessing; betrayal brings the curse of divine judgment. This element of the covenant was picked up later by the great prophets of Israel.

CHOSEN FOR SERVICE

It is important to see how the Exodus story ties in with the dramatic sequence of the Book of Genesis. As we saw in the last study, Genesis 1–3 gives a word picture of the fundamental human situation: the estrangement of humanity from God in spite of humanity's supreme position as God's representative on earth. The consequences of the human tragedy are spelled out in the stories of Genesis 4–11, in which things go from bad to worse. Then we are told in Gen 12:1-3 that God, to meet this universal human predicament, took appropriate action by calling a man (Abraham) and promising him that his people would be the means of blessing to all the broken and divided families of humankind. The God who speaks to Moses is "the God of the ancestors"—that is, Abraham, Isaac, and Jacob and Sarah, Rebekah, Leah, and Rachel. Thus the deliverance of the

Israelites from Egyptian bondage is seen in the perspective of God's redemptive concern to bring all people to the full measure of humanity intended in the creation.

Questions to Think About

1. Some religions (such as Hinduism and Taoism) maintain that Ultimate Reality is unnameable; attempts to name God reduce the divine to the level of human distinctions or domesticate the divine in the temporal realm of change and decay. Against this view, how would you understand the story of the giving of God's name to Moses and the people?

2. Does it make sense in our time to say that "God acts in history"? What meaning does Exod 3:7-8 have for oppressed and exploited peoples today?

3. A justice of the Supreme Court defended a decision by saying that in modern society "there are no absolutes." How does a "situational ethic" square with the covenant faith? Would you say that all of the Ten Commandments are absolutely binding in every situation?

4. "Thou shalt have no other gods before me." What does God's "jealousy" mean in our situation? What are some of the "gods" that people worship today?

5. A fundamental premise of the Bible, both Old and New Testaments, is that God has "chosen" a people for service. According to your present understanding, discuss the meaning of the election of Israel (or the church).

Suggestions for Further Reading

Anderson, Bernhard W. *Contours of Old Testament Theology.* Minneapolis: Fortress Press, 1999.

————. *Understanding the Old Testament.* 5th ed. (with S. Bishop and J. Newman). Upper Saddle River, N.J.: Pearson Prentice Hall, 2006. See chapter 1, "The Beginnings of Israel," and chapter 2, "Liberation from Bondage."

Childs, Brevard. *The Book of Exodus.* Old Testament Library. Philadelphia: Westminster, 1974. Stresses the place of the Book of Exodus in the biblical canon.

Clements, Ronald E. *Exodus.* Cambridge Commentary on the New English Bible. Cambridge: Cambridge University Press, 1972. Very helpful.

Fackenheim, Emil L. *God's Presence in History: Jewish Affirmations and Philosophical Reflections.* New York: Harper and Row, 1970. A profound discussion of Exodus and Sinai in Jewish tradition.

Harrelson, Walter. *The Ten Commandments and Human Rights.* Macon, Ga.: Mercer University Press, 1997; orig. publ. Philadelphia: Fortress Press, 1978.

Hillers, Delbert R. *Covenant: The History of a Biblical Idea.* Baltimore: Johns Hopkins University Press, 1969. A clearly written, illuminating discussion.

Lohfink, Norbert F. *Option for the Poor: The Basic Principle of Liberation Theology in Light of the Bible.* North Richland Hills, Tex.: Bibal, 1996. An illuminating discussion by a prominent Roman Catholic biblical scholar.

Mendenhall, George E. *Ancient Israel's Faith and History: An Introduction to the Bible in Context.* Edited by Gary Herion. Philadelphia: Westminster John Knox, 2001. Introduces the Ancient Near Eastern setting of the Hebrew Bible, with particular attention to archaeological evidence.

———. "Covenant." In *Anchor Bible Dictionary* 2:1179–1202. Edited by David Noel Freedman. Garden City, N.Y.: Doubleday, 1992.

———. *Law and Covenant in Israel and the Ancient Near East.* Pittsburgh: Biblical Colloquium, 1955. A pioneering and still relevant study of Israel's covenant tradition in the light of Hittite parallels.

Miller, Patrick D. *The God You Have: Politics and the First Commandment.* Philadelphia: Fortress Press, 2004. Discusses modern forms of idolatry in light of the first commandment.

Moberly, R. W. L. *At the Mountain of God: Story and Theology in Exodus 32–34. Journal for the Study of the Old Testament,* Suppl. 22. Sheffield, England: JSOT Press, 1983.

The Discipline of Disaster

Study Passages

1. Jeremiah 1:4-19
   Appointed to Be a Messenger
2. Jeremiah 2:1-13
   Covenant Lawsuit against Israel
3. Jeremiah 7:1-15
   The Temple as a Den of Thieves
4. Jeremiah 31:31-34
   The New Covenant

This is a study in tragedy. During Jeremiah's long career as a prophet in Jerusalem (626–587 BCE), events moved swiftly and inexorably toward the precipice of disaster. The very foundations shook under the shattering impact of ominous historical events. And finally the curtain of the first main act of the biblical drama came down on a scene of utter ruin: the temple was destroyed, the nation had fallen, and the cream of the population had been carried away into foreign exile. "By the waters of Babylon, there we sat down and wept, when we remembered Zion [Jerusalem]," lamented a psalmist (Ps 137:1).

THE PEOPLE THAT WALKED IN DARKNESS

To appreciate the full pathos of the tragedy, let us telescope Israel's history from the Exodus to the fall of the nation into a short summary. After the miraculous deliverance from Egypt, the Israelites were forged into a community in the experiences of the desert, where, despite their murmurings, they repeatedly experienced the grace and the faithfulness of God (Exodus 16–18; Numbers 10–36). With a sense of God-given destiny, kept alive through the memory of the saving event of the Exodus and the covenant of Sinai, they moved into the Promised Land. There, under the leadership of Joshua and his successors, they successfully maintained a foothold despite enemy pressure. For some generations the people were bound together in a tribal confederacy known as Israel. During this period (the two centuries before David) the people came together periodically on occasions of worship to renew their covenantal allegiance to the God who had shown benevolent power in the Exodus. As on the occasion of the great convocation at Shechem under Joshua (Joshua 24), they heard anew the marvelous story of what God had done, they listened to the public reading of the stipulations of the covenant, and they renewed their vow to serve the God of the Exodus and to obey the covenant laws. The formula of Exod 24:7 was echoed in these services of covenant renewal: "All that the Lord has spoken we will do, and we will be obedient."

In time, the community Israel became a nation and under the leadership of David rose to a height of prestige and glory. In some circles, this new development was regarded as the continuation and outcome of what God had started to do in the period of the Exodus. Royal theologians advanced the view that God had entered into a special covenant with Israel *through David* the king, a covenant that guaranteed social stability and the continuity of the Davidic dynasty (2 Samuel 7).[1] The story of God's saving actions, begun in the Exodus, was seen to point toward the special choice of David and of the temple on Mount Zion in the divine purpose (see Psalm 78, especially verses 67-72). In other words, God was continuing to lead the people into the future.

Troubles soon broke out, however. Under the oppressive reign of David's son Solomon there was great restiveness beneath the surface of the nation's glory, and at Solomon's death the volcano of revolution erupted. The once-united kingdom was split into North and South by civil strife, with the North clinging to the Mosaic tradition and the South emphasizing the covenant with David. The people of Israel, torn apart by fratricidal rivalry and warfare, were soon caught in the power struggle of the ancient Near East. Crushed beneath the heel of the conqueror, the Northern Kingdom was destroyed by the Assyrians in 722 BCE, and the Southern Kingdom was finished off by the Babylonians in the fateful year of 587 BCE.

THE CONTEMPORANEITY OF THE COVENANT

During this tumultuous period, there appeared a remarkable succession of prophets—individuals like Samuel, Elijah, Amos, Hosea, Isaiah, Jeremiah, and Ezekiel. In all ancient history there was nothing else that matched the succession of prophets who arose in Israel. Today many people suppose that a prophet is a clairvoyant who peers into a crystal ball, as it were, and discloses the shape of things to come. This, however, is a caricature of prophecy.

The true prophet was one who interpreted the meaning of the historical crisis in the light of Israel's covenant loyalty. The prophets were not extremists who introduced radically new conceptions that broke with the past, nor were they reactionaries who merely repeated the old traditions in a new time. Rather, they spoke to the urgent and imperative present of the community by reinterpreting the meaning of the covenant traditions in the present crisis and by warning the people of the consequences of their action for the future.[2]

The tense that matters most in Israel's faith is the present, the *today* of the covenant. This contemporaneous note, frequently heard on occasions of worship in the Israelite community ("O that today you would hearken to his voice" [Ps 95:7]) is sounded in a passage in Deuteronomy that serves as an introduction to the Decalogue:

> The Lord our God made a covenant with us in Horeb [Sinai].

Not with our ancestors did the Lord make this covenant,
but with us, who are all of us here alive this day.
(Deut 5:2-3)

If the prophets speak to us today, it is because in our time the
present is qualitatively the same, even though the date is in the
twenty-first century.

THE TRIAL OF ISRAEL

For this study we have arbitrarily selected Jeremiah as representative of the prophetic movement and a few passages from the Book
of Jeremiah as representative of this prophet's message.[3] During
his career (about 626–587 BCE), Jeremiah saw the colossal Assyrian empire disintegrate. He witnessed the intense nationalism of
the Southern Kingdom, fanned by the patriotic hope for independence. He beheld the new Babylonian empire rise from the ashes
of Assyria and spread destruction throughout Palestine. What
was the meaning of these events? Like prophets who preceded
him (for instance, Hosea in the middle of the eighth century BCE),
Jeremiah insisted that disaster was a form of discipline—that God
was "teaching" the people through these tragic events (as the word
"discipline" literally suggests). God was actively confronting the
people on the plane of history, leading them through suffering
to a new beginning in divine grace. Therefore, even though there
was tragedy, it was meaningful tragedy.

The selected passages form a good sequence for discussion.
The first one (Jer 1:4-19) describes Jeremiah's commission in
a dialogue that reminds us of the account of Moses's call. The
prophet understands himself to be a messenger who is summoned and sent, who speaks not his own opinions but the message of his Lord. Hence the frequent messenger formula: "Thus
saith the Lord" (see Gen 32:3-5 for the secular use of the messenger form of speech). Verse 10 is important. Notice that the
first effect of God's Word, spoken through the prophetic messenger, is destructive: it "roots up and pulls down." Only after this

negative or critical function has been performed does it "build and plant." This calls our attention to a characteristic emphasis of the prophetic message: to know God, or rather to be known by God, is to be exposed to divine judgment. God sets a plumb line against the unjust structures of society (Amos 7:7-9) and searches the innermost motives of the heart (Ps 139:1-6). There is no dark corner where the searchlight of God's criticism does not reach.

The second passage (Jer 2:1-13), which contains the message of the prophetic messenger (note the messenger formula in 2:1-2 and 2:4-5a), belongs to a literary genre known as the "covenant lawsuit."[4] The prophet, acting as a prosecuting lawyer who represents God's court, reviews the history of Israel in the light of the covenant commitment. Viewed from this standpoint, it is a long history of ingratitude and unfaithfulness to the God who has graciously delivered the people from bondage and brought them into a good land. The past is reviewed not for its own sake but to understand the meaning of the present. The people preferred to live on their own terms, following the idols of their own hearts. The indictment comes to a resounding climax in verse 13, where the prophet accuses the people of rejecting the God who is "the fountain of living waters," to hew out for themselves "broken cisterns that can hold no water." This is reminiscent of the theme we have met previously in the paradise story (see STUDY I).

The third passage strikes at the very heart of the popular belief, encouraged by royal-covenant theology, that the temple is the sign of God's presence with the people. Jeremiah's "temple sermon," which Jesus later referred to (Mark 11:17), is a hard-hitting criticism of religion—that is, of the kind of religion that is the tool of the status quo or "establishment" and the justification of accepted social values or priorities. The prophet warns worshipers against supposing that they are safe if they "go to church" while their society violates the human dignity of persons and thereby shouts defiance at the sovereignty of God. The temple is not a cave where robbers can find refuge to count their spoil! Notice the "ifs" of the conditional Mosaic covenant (verses

5-7) and the specific citation of some of the commandments of the Decalogue (verses 8-10). The blessings of the covenant sanction a lifestyle that shows fidelity to God's demands, but the curses (judgments) of the covenant come inescapably upon a false way of life. The ancient shrine of the old tribal confederacy, once located at Shiloh (1 Sam 1:3), had been destroyed without trace by the Philistines, and, says Jeremiah, a similar fate will befall the proud temple of Jerusalem. For God is the critic, not the defender, of an unjust social order. On the basis of the covenant, God enters into controversy with the people.

JUDGMENT IN HISTORY

In his time Jeremiah perceived that the historical crisis disclosed the judgment of God, and he summoned people to repent, or amend their way of life, while there was still time. Indeed, he insisted that God was using the Babylonian invader to shock the people to their senses so that they might turn from pursuing the "devices and desires of their own hearts"—to use the words of a familiar prayer—and find the true peace and security of covenant relationship with God. In some respects, Jeremiah's message was like that of Isaiah, who in the latter part of the eighth century BCE boldly described the Assyrian foe as the "rod of the Lord's anger" that was being used to discipline a rebellious people (Isa 10:5-19).[5]

It comes down to this: People are free to choose their course of action, but they are not free to escape the consequences of that action as long as God is actively present "with us" in judgment and in mercy. The God for whom the prophets of Israel speak is the Holy One who acts to overthrow systems of exploitation, to humble the proud and exalt those of low degree, and to shatter the false gods (loyalties, values) in which people place their trust. There is, according to the modern historian Herbert Butterfield, a discernible element of judgment in human history.[6] But the end of this shock treatment is that human beings may be brought to their senses, may become more fully human in their relationships, and at last may find their true community in a new covenant with God. This is the theme of the final study passage (Jer 31:31-34), from which the New Testament takes its name.[7]

Questions to Think About

1. Karl Marx observed that the beginning of all criticism is the criticism of religion. Jeremiah, though speaking from the standpoint of faith in God, would have agreed. Why?

2. Make a list of some of the "broken cisterns" (compare Jer 2:13) in which moderns have placed their trust. Would you include education, science, psychology, technology, communism, the "American way," organized religion?

3. In his second inaugural address, Abraham Lincoln said, "If God will that [the Civil War] continue until every drop of blood drawn by the taskmaster's lash shall be repaid with two drawn by the sword . . . then . . . 'the judgments of the Lord are true and righteous altogether.'" Does our present historical crisis disclose the judgment of God? How should this view affect our attitude as citizens?

4. Discuss the widely held view that religion belongs in one sphere and political and economic issues in another. Would Jeremiah have agreed with the policy of keeping social issues out of the pulpit?

5. Jeremiah believed that God was working through an unbeliever, Nebuchadrezzar, to accomplish the divine purpose in history. What do you think Jeremiah's attitude would have been today toward radical forces of revolution in the world? Toward the use of military force to spread democracy?

6. Suppose that Western civilization should fall, as the Roman Empire collapsed in the time of Augustine. How would a biblical prophet interpret this disaster?

Suggestions for Further Reading

Anderson, Bernhard W. *The Eighth Century Prophets: Amos, Hosea, Isaiah, Micah.* Eugene, Ore.: Wipf and Stock, 2003; orig. publ. Philadelphia: Fortress Press, 1978.

———. *Understanding the Old Testament.* 5th ed. (with S. Bishop and J. Newman). Upper Saddle River, N.J.: Pearson Prentice Hall, 2006. See the detailed discussion of the prophetic movement starting in chapter 8, "The Prophetic Troublers of Israel," and continuing through chapter 12, "The Doom of the Nation."

Bright, John. *Jeremiah.* Anchor Bible. Garden City, N.Y.: Doubleday, 1965. A fresh translation with helpful introduction and notes.

Brueggemann, Walter. *A Commentary on Jeremiah: Exile and Homecoming.* Grand Rapids, Mich.: Eerdmans, 1998.

———. *The Prophetic Imagination.* Rev. ed. Minneapolis: Fortress Press, 2001.

Heschel, Abraham Joshua. *The Prophets.* New York: Harper and Row, 1963. A foundational work by a Jewish philosopher.

Holladay, William A. *Jeremiah: A Fresh Reading.* New York: Pilgrim, 1990.

———. *Jeremiah.* Hermeneia. 2 vols. Philadelphia: Fortress Press, 1986, 1989.

Rad, Gerhard von. *The Message of the Prophets.* New York: Harper and Row, 1965.

A New **Exodus**

Study Passages

1. Isaiah 40:1-11
   A Herald of Good News
2. Isaiah 42:5-17; 43:14-21
   The Divine Surprise
3. Isaiah 52:12—53:13
   The Suffering Servant
4. Isaiah 55:1-13
   Promises of the Everlasting Covenant

We come now to the second main phase of the biblical drama. The scene opens in Babylonia, to which country Judeans or Jews[1] had been deported during the capture of the city of Jerusalem. Many of these displaced persons had settled down in relative prosperity and security in the foreign land, but the vision of Jerusalem, destroyed and impoverished, could not be erased from their memories (see Psalm 137). To them, the terrible thing was not just the physical calamity but the religious despair and disillusionment that the fall of Jerusalem had occasioned. Jerusalem was not an ordinary city to them. It was a center of historical meaning—meaning that had been disclosed when God delivered the Israelites from Egypt and providentially guided their history to its greatest fulfillment in the establishment of the dynasty of David.[2] Yet the poignant question inevitably arose: If God had made unbreakable promises of grace to David and had designated Jerusalem as the central place of worship, why did God allow a terrible calamity to occur that brought the Davidic line to an end and destroyed the temple? The anguish of this question, raised in a time of national distress, is vividly expressed in Psalm 89, particularly in the lament with which it concludes (verses 38-51).

A SPIRITUAL BLACKOUT

The crisis of the fall of Jerusalem was experienced intensely by the people of the Southern Kingdom (Judah) who shared the covenant theology associated with King David (see STUDY III). Southern interpreters maintained that the climax of Israel's sacred history was God's choice of David to be king and of the temple of Zion (Jerusalem) to be God's "dwelling place" (Psalms 78, 132). It was their conviction that God made an "everlasting covenant" with David and his line (Psalm 89) and set aside Jerusalem with its temple as the "city of God" (Psalms 46, 84). This theological view provided a guarantee of social stability amid the disorders of history, when every change of administration was an opportunity for disruptive, chaotic forces to break loose.

The fall of Jerusalem was thus a spiritual blackout, especially for those who identified God's purpose in history with the preservation of the Davidic state. Jeremiah 28 provides a vivid description of the tension between nationalism and faith, between popular prophecy and true prophecy. The popular prophet had declared, "God is with us" (the meaning of the Hebrew word *immanuel*), and, therefore, no evil can come upon us. But the genuine prophet had said, "God is with us," and, therefore, all securities—Jerusalem, the temple, organized religion, the nation—stand under divine judgment. It is easy to see how those who had been beguiled by popular prophecy would have concluded that God had "let them down" when Jerusalem was destroyed. It seemed that the whole history of God's covenant with Israel was a history of failure!

But the God who in the past led a dispirited band of slaves out of Egypt was about to open a way into the future once again. This is the testimony of a series of magnificent poems found in the latter part of the Book of Isaiah (chapters 40–55). Speaking to despairing exiles in Babylonia, the poet announces the good news that the God of Israel, who controls the destinies of all nations, will accomplish the return of the Israelites to their homeland, where they will take their part in the fulfillment of the divine purpose for history. Strikingly, this prophet resorts to the imagery of the exodus from Egypt to describe Israel's new "going out" from captivity and the opening of a new way into the future (Isa 44:27; 43:16-17; 51:10-11; compare Exod 14:15-31). It is appropriate, then, to speak of this event as the "New Exodus."[3]

THE ECUMENICAL PURPOSE OF GOD

It is widely recognized that the last part of our present Book of Isaiah comes from a follower of the prophet Isaiah, who about two centuries later—in the time of the Exile—reinterpreted the message of his master. This "unknown prophet of the Exile" is usually called "Second Isaiah" to distinguish him from Isaiah of Jerusalem (740–700 BCE), whose prophecies are found in the first section of the Book of Isaiah (chapters 1–39).

In the time of Second Isaiah the Babylonian empire was declining, and the political news on the international scene was the rise of a ruler named Cyrus (Isa 44:28; 45:1). Having established control over the Medes and the Persians (about 550 BCE), Cyrus marched into the heart of the Babylonian empire, and in 538 Babylon fell. Second Isaiah was active in the period between the rise of the new conqueror and the final capitulation of Babylon—that is, between 550 and 538 BCE. An enlightened monarch, Cyrus granted captive peoples the right to live in their own countries and to carry on their own traditions. Small wonder that many people who groaned under the heavy yoke of Babylonia looked to him as a messianic liberator! This is the life situation to which the "unknown prophet" spoke. His task as a prophetic messenger was not just to predict the imminent downfall of Babylon and the release of captives but to interpret the religious meaning of this momentous event.

The best way to prepare for this study is to read through all fifteen chapters of Second Isaiah (Isaiah 40–55) in a modern translation. From a purely literary point of view, this is poetry at its finest. From a theological viewpoint, these poems represent the crowning maturity of the faith of Israel. The passages selected set forth themes that are elaborated with symphonic splendor in the prophet's work as a whole. The central thrust of the prophetic message is that world events do not happen by caprice but are embraced within the overruling sovereignty of God, the Creator and Redeemer, to whom Israel's historical traditions bear witness.

A HERALD OF GOOD NEWS

Like a prologue, the first passage (Isa 40:1-11) sets the tone of the whole series of poems. The prophet (who appears in the "I" of verse 6) senses that he has stood, as it were, within the heavenly council where God was heard issuing a decree to be announced to Israel—and to the whole world. A key word in this section is "good news" (verse 9; compare 52:7), the word that reappears in the New Testament as "gospel." What is the content of this good news? It is this: God is about to act, just as at the beginning of Israel's history God took the initiative to deliver a people from a no-exit situation and to open a way through the wilderness into a promised future. To an unbeliever, perhaps, there would be nothing extraordinary in the return of exiles to their homeland. But to those who viewed this event in the perspective of the Exodus and the whole Israelite tradition, this would be a theophany—a manifestation of the glory of God on the stage of history:

> Behold, the Lord GOD comes with might,
>   and his arm rules for him. . . .
> He will feed his flock like a shepherd,
>   he will gather the lambs in his arms,
> he will carry them in his bosom,
>   and gently lead those that are with young.
>   (Isa 40:10-11; compare 52:7-10)

In the prophet's ecstatic faith, the historical drama was moving toward the dawn of a new age under God's rule, the "kingdom of God." It is significant that at the beginning of the third stage of the biblical drama John the Baptist recapitulates the theme of this chapter (compare Isa 40:3 with Mark 1:3).

One of the central themes of the prophet's message is the *novelty* of God's action in history (Isa 42:5-17; 43:14-21). Life is not merely lived within the order of nature with its recurring rhythms of "seedtime and harvest, cold and heat, summer and winter, day and night" (Gen 8:22), but is caught up in a purposive movement of historical events that are new, unique, and unrepeatable. The nations, when brought to trial, are unable to testify to this divine purpose in which the startling developments under Cyrus are related to the "former things" (the call of Abraham, the exodus from Egypt, the march through the wilderness to the Promised Land). But Israel, out of its own life story, bears witness to the God whose purpose spans the ages, from beginning to end.

At times, the prophet seems to stress the newness of God's action so sharply that the past is to be forgotten:

> Remember not the former things,
>   nor consider the things of old,
> Behold, I am doing a new thing;
>   now it springs forth, do you not perceive it?
>   (Isa 43:18-19)

Yet the prophet is equally insistent that Israel should "remember the former things of old" (Isa 46:8-11). These statements are not contradictory when one considers the creative manner in which the prophet reinterprets the old traditions so that they are convincingly relevant to the present situation in which the community finds itself. Here the Israelite tradition is not just a past memory but provides the imagery for understanding the new thing that God is doing, the new word that he is speaking. Again and again, the prophet resorts to the tradition of the exodus from Egypt to describe the new exodus of salvation. The prophet is not talking, however, about a repetition of the first exodus. Rather, the imagery of the old is used poetically to express the divine surprise that is about to occur.

THE SERVANT OF GOD

According to Second Isaiah, Israel is God's "Servant" (Isa 41:8-10; 43:8-13; 44:1-2). This Servant is blind, deaf, and stubborn. Still, despite his weaknesses, the Servant has been chosen for a unique role in the accomplishment of God's historical purpose. God had an ulterior motive in delivering Israel from Babylonian bondage: that Israel might be a "light to the nations" (42:6; compare 49:6). Here the prophet understands profoundly the meaning of the call of Abraham and Sarah to be a blessing to the families of the earth (Gen 12:1-3):

> Look to the rock from which you were hewn,
>   and to the quarry from which you were dug.
> Look to Abraham your father
>   and to Sarah who bore you;
> for when he was but one I called him,
>   and I blessed him and made him many.
>   (Isa 51:1-2)

This theme is developed with sublime grandeur in our third passage (Isa 52:12—53:13), which belongs to a series of special "servant poems."[4] In this passage, one of the most important in the whole Old Testament, the "Suffering Servant" is portrayed in the guise of an individual. At the beginning and end of the poem (52:13-15; 53:10-13), God speaks, announcing the exaltation of the Servant. In the central portion (53:1-9), the representatives of the nations testify. They have come to realize that the meaning of Israel's suffering was not merely that the people had experienced the discipline of divine judgment. That was part of the matter, to be sure, but there was a much deeper truth. The Servant's suffering was vicarious—that is, was borne for others.

Through the Servant's affliction, the peoples were made whole, restored to health, "justified" or brought into right relationship with God and with one another. This is the most astounding testimony of the Bible: that God chooses the way of humiliation, suffering, rejection, and defeat to make known divine glory and triumph in the world. And this is the truth that is fulfilled and "made flesh" in the New Testament.

THE PROMISES OF GRACE

The final chapter (Isa 55:1-13) rounds off the prophet's message by sounding again the theme of unconditional pardon and grace heard at the beginning. A free-for-all invitation is given to God's banquet table. Here the startling announcement is made that the unconditional covenant of grace, once made with David according to royal theology (2 Samuel 7), is now extended to *the people* (Isa 55:3). The covenant relationship with God is not based upon obedience to legal stipulations, as in the Mosaic covenant, but is grounded solely upon the grace of God, whose thoughts are not our thoughts and whose ways are not our ways. God makes an "everlasting covenant" with the people, like the covenant with Noah whose sign is the rainbow in the clouds (54:9-10; compare Gen 9:8-17). This covenant of grace, which is central to the gospel of the New Testament, does not relieve human beings of responsibility. Rather, it provides the motive for turning from evil ways and unworthy thoughts and returning to the God whose mercy is immeasurable and whose ways exceed human comprehension (Isa 55:6-9).

Questions to Think About

1. Contrast Second Isaiah's understanding of history with the nihilistic view that history has no ultimate meaning and that we must find only our own temporary meanings. What are the grounds for saying that all human history from beginning to end is embraced within a single purpose?

2. How does the prophet's announcement that God is "doing a new thing" speak to our time? Does this demand a break with past tradition and a radically new theology?

3. Compare the Mosaic covenant and its conditional stipulations ("If . . . then") with the "everlasting covenant," which is grounded solely in divine grace (pardon, forgiveness). Do you think that a greater emphasis upon divine grace undercuts the motive for human action and responsibility?

4. How does Second Isaiah view the "election" or call of Israel as having a special role in the divine purpose? How do you account for the "mystery of Israel"—the people that have survived through the centuries to the present?

5. Consider the vocation of the church as the "new Israel." Does the church participate in the mystery of the Suffering Servant?

6. Muslims trace their religious history to Abraham through his son Ishmael. What might this mean for Jews, Muslims, and Christians today?

Suggestions for Further Reading

Anderson, Bernhard W. *Contours of Old Testament Theology.* Minneapolis: Fortress Press, 1999. See especially chapter 32, "Prophecy in a New Idiom."

————. "Exodus Typology in Second Isaiah." In *Israel's Prophetic Heritage.* Edited by B. W. Anderson and Walter J. Harrelson. New York: Harper and Row, 1962.

————. *Understanding the Old Testament.* 5th ed. (with S. Bishop and J. Newman). Upper Saddle River, N.J.: Pearson Prentice Hall, 2006. See especially chapter 14, "The Dawn of a New Age."

Blenkinsopp, Joseph. *Isaiah 40–55.* Anchor Bible Commentary. Garden City, N.Y.: Doubleday, 2002.

Childs, Brevard. *Isaiah.* Old Testament Library. Philadelphia: Westminster, 2001.

LeClerc, Thomas L. *Yahweh Is Exalted in Justice: Solidarity and Conflict in Isaiah.* Minneapolis: Fortress Press, 2001.

McKenzie, John L. *Second Isaiah.* Anchor Bible. Garden City, N.Y.: Doubleday, 1968. A fresh translation with helpful introduction and notes by a Roman Catholic scholar.

Muilenberg, James. "Introduction and Exegesis to Isaiah 40–66." In *Interpreter's Bible.* Nashville: Abingdon, 1956. An excellent commentary.

Westermann, Claus. *Isaiah 40–66.* Old Testament Library. Philadelphia: Westminster, 1969.

The **People** of the **Torah**

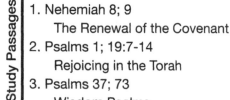

Study Passages

1. Nehemiah 8; 9
   The Renewal of the Covenant
2. Psalms 1; 19:7-14
   Rejoicing in the Torah
3. Psalms 37; 73
   Wisdom Psalms
4. Job (at least the following)
   Prose prologue (1:1—2:13)
   Job's lament (chapter 3)
   Part of the first cycle of speeches (chapters 4–14)
   Job's final defense (especially chapter 31)
   The voice from the whirlwind (chapter 38)
   Job's repentance (42:1-6)
   Prose epilogue (42:7-17)

This brings us to one of the most important—though for many Christians the most problematic—phases of the biblical drama. The spotlight falls on Ezra and Nehemiah, two men who played a decisive role in the re-formation of Israel into the community known as Judaism. The religious phenomenon called Judaism emerged during the period after the exile when "Jews" (former residents of Judah) returned to Palestine. It was characterized by devotion to the Mosaic Torah (the Pentateuch) as the constitutional basis of life and thought.

Someone has said that Israel went into exile as a nation and returned as a church. The word "Judaism" refers to a new stage in the biblical drama: Israel was no longer a state but a religious community, somewhat analogous to the time before David when the people were united in a tribal confederacy on the basis of covenant allegiance. This worshiping community was like an ellipse with two centers: the Temple and the Torah.

A NEW BEGINNING

To see this in proper perspective, we need to resume the story from the time of Second Isaiah, almost a century earlier than the period of Ezra. Shortly after Babylon capitulated to the Persian army, Cyrus issued an edict allowing Jews the privilege of returning to their homeland. So Jewish exiles began their homeward trek to Zion (Jerusalem). When they arrived, they found everything in ruins: the Temple was destroyed, the walls of Jerusalem were leveled, the city was desolate. Nevertheless, inspired by the prophecies of Haggai and Zechariah, they set about rebuilding the Temple, a project that was completed about 515 BCE.

Then Ezra came onto the scene, according to the sequence of events given by the historian who wrote the Books of Chronicles, Ezra, and Nehemiah. With the permission of the Persian king, Ezra led a caravan of Jews back to Palestine around the middle of the fifth century BCE, or slightly later. Most important, he brought with him a copy of "the book of the law [*torah*] of Moses" (probably the Pentateuch, the so-called Five Books of Moses), and he lost no time in convening the people to hear the reading of its contents. One of the solemn moments in Israel's history is described in Nehemiah 8 and 9, a great occasion of covenant renewal. The ceremony included the public reading of the Torah to the people, the offering of a penitential prayer that summarized God's gracious dealings with the people throughout their historical pilgrimage, and the covenant pledge of the people "to walk in God's law [*torah*], which was given by Moses the servant of God." The event is to be compared with the covenant-renewal ceremony led by Joshua (Joshua 24) or by King Josiah (2 Kings 23).

At about the same time, Nehemiah, a cupbearer to the Persian king, received permission to return to Palestine as a Persian governor of Judah. After a memorable midnight tour around the city walls of Jerusalem, he organized the Jews for work, and in less than two months the walls were rebuilt, despite hostile resistance. Thus, under the religious leadership of Ezra and the statesmanship of Nehemiah, the "congregation of Israel" received a new lease on life. It seemed as though the glowing promises spoken by prophets like Second Isaiah were on the verge of fulfillment.[1]

COVENANT RENEWAL

The vitality of Judaism is indicated by the great amount of biblical literature that comes from the period following the exile. The Pentateuch (the first five books of the Old Testament) received its final form in this period. Indeed, the whole Old Testament as we have received it is stamped indelibly with the way of life and thought characteristic of the time. In this study we can do little more than scratch the surface of biblical Judaism, the stage of Israel's historical pilgrimage out of which Christianity emerged in the fullness of time.

The best way to prepare for this study is to familiarize oneself with the account of Ezra's career as it is related in Ezra 7–8; Nehemiah 8–10; and Ezra 9–10 (the chapters should be read in that order). In these chapters you will find an emphasis on ritual, or "priestly" matters, which loom large in long sections of the Pentateuch, as well as a concern for maintaining the purity of the faith by rigid laws against mixed marriages. Above all, attention should be given to the account of Ezra's reading of the Torah (Neh 8:1-8) and the solemn liturgical prayer that followed (Neh 9:6-38).

Notice that the prayer strikes a note characteristic of Israel's faith from the first. It is a summary of the "mighty acts of God" by which Israel had been brought onto the stage of history with a unique vocation and destiny. Penitently, the people acknowledge that the Exile was God's judgment on their covenant unfaithfulness. Gratefully, they rejoice in the new exodus from Babylonian captivity. Solemnly, they vow to renew the covenant by obeying the stipulations of the Torah. This is one of the great confessions of faith in the Old Testament. Unlike Israel's early creedal confession (Deut 26:5-9), the recital of God's saving acts begins with the creation, as does the "salvation history" or "storytelling" in Psalm 136, which probably comes from this period. We have already found this spacious perspective in the message of Second Isaiah, which was addressed to "the people in whose heart is [God's] law" (Isa 51:7). And in the portrayal of the consummation found in Isa 2:1-5 (Mic 4:1-4) the peoples of the world stream to Jerusalem, from which God's *torah*, or Word, goes forth. Thus the Torah discloses the meaning of all history and creation.

REJOICING IN THE TORAH

From the great amount of literature from the period of Judaism, we have selected for special study some of the psalms of Israel and some of the writings from Israel's wisdom movement. The Book of Psalms is so important in Jewish and Christian worship that it would call for a special study all by itself.[2] Like modern hymn-books, it reflects a long history of worship in which songs of various types are included: hymns of praise (for example, Psalm 103), laments and confessions of sin (Psalms 22, 51), thanksgivings (Psalm 118), and songs for use on special occasions (Psalm 47, a New Year's psalm). The final edition of the Book of Psalms, however, is a product of the period of Judaism and is appropriately arranged in five books like the Pentateuch itself. The hymnbook is introduced with two psalms that set forth the cardinal tenets of Judaism: Psalm 1, which glorifies the study of God's Torah (see also Ps 19:7-14), and Psalm 2, which in this period— as in the time of the New Testament—was understood to refer to the Messiah (see also Psalm 110). Thus these introductory psalms invite readers "to choose the right path to the Messianic glory: the study of the law and obedience toward the word of God."[3]

After becoming familiarized with the Ezra story, turn to Psalm 1. This psalm draws a distinction between two kinds of persons: the "God-fearer," who delights in God's Torah day and night and who therefore is like a tree whose roots are nourished by life-giving waters, and the "wicked" person or the "fool" (Ps 14:1), who vainly lives by self-chosen standards, without dependence upon God. Remember that when the Israelites thought of God's "law," they did not think of a heavenly police officer who coldly enforces statutes. Rather, they confessed their relationship to the God who had graciously redeemed Israel from bondage and had given them "teaching" or "direction" (the proper translation of the Hebrew word *torah*) in the way they should walk. From the very first, the covenant and the Torah were linked together. As time went on, many "laws" were added to the covenant tradition, and, under Ezra, the Torah was identified especially with the Pentateuch, or Five Books of Moses. You would think that obeying the many instructions of this Torah would be burdensome. But reading the Torah psalms (Pss 1; 19:7-14; 119) will disclose that Judaism found God's Torah a delight, "rejoicing the heart" (Ps 19:8). The chief concern was that of glorifying God in all daily actions and relationships:

> Oh, how I love your law [*torah*]!
> It is my meditation all the day.
> Your commandment makes me wiser than my enemies,
> for it is always with me.
>
> (Ps 119:97-98)

THE BEGINNING OF WISDOM

Ezra's great reform had its strengths—but also had great dangers that were evident to those who reflected deeply upon the sufferings and imbalances of life. It is one thing to delight in God's will. It is another to be so self-righteously sure of what God's will is in a specific situation that one thanks God that one is not as other people (see the parable of the Pharisee and the publican, Luke 18:9-14).

Perhaps modern churches and synagogues fall into this danger insofar as a code of "thou shalts" and "thou shalt nots" is set forth as the standard of virtue—as do leaders who self-righteously claim that God is on their side in the international struggle and that their enemies are the wicked who fall short of the glory of God. According to Israel's prophets, God's will brought the people under judgment—God had a controversy with Israel. If we think seriously about how impossible it is to stand before God on the basis of moral goodness (Ps 130:3), perhaps we can anticipate why the Christian gospel protests against all legalism and moralism and puts our relation with God on an entirely different basis from the *torah*, or "law" (Gal 2:11-21).

The belief of Judaism, however, was that God's Torah is not just "law" but also the beginning of wisdom, as we can see from a wisdom psalm like Psalm 37 (see especially verses 30-31). Wisdom, therefore, is not a human achievement but a gift bestowed by God, one that inspires humility and reverence:

> Truly, the fear of the LORD, that is wisdom;
> and to depart from evil is understanding.
> (Job 28:28)

Those who have this sort of faith may reach understanding; those who fail at this starting point are "fools" who grope in ignorance.

THE VOICE FROM THE WHIRLWIND

Some of Israel's sages pushed their search for understanding into the mystery of God's creation and even dared to raise questions about the justice of God's ways. This is the case in the Book of Job, one of the greatest literary contributions of Israel's wisdom movement. The author of this work has been aptly called the "Shakespeare of the Old Testament."

Ideally, for this study unit the whole Book of Job should be read. At least read the selected portions recommended at the beginning of this chapter. Notice that an old folk tale, written in prose, now stands as the prologue and epilogue to a poetic work that consists of Job's lament (chapter 3), his conversation with his friends in three rounds (chapters 4–27), his final oath of innocence (chapters 29–31), God's answer out of the whirlwind (chapters 38–41), and Job's repentance (42:1-6; compare 40:1-5). The author has used the old tale as a "framing device," inserting his poetry into this envelope for the purpose of dramatic contrast.[4]

The Job of the story is a traditional righteous person, "blameless and upright, an individual who feared God, and turned away from evil"—one who bears adversity with calm patience and long-suffering. The Job of the poem, however, refuses to suffer the "slings and arrows of outrageous fortune" meekly and without protest. Not only does Job challenge his three orthodox friends, who steadfastly insist that his suffering has been brought about by some sin, but he also dares to expostulate with God and even to accuse God of maladministration of justice on earth. Finally, after an overwhelming demonstration of God's wisdom and power as Creator (the Voice from the whirlwind), Job acknowledges that he has no grounds on which to challenge the Almighty and repents of his presumptuous speech.

Various questions will come to mind in reading the book. What is the real problem with which Job wrestles? Why can he not accept the "pastoral counseling" of his friends? Is the Voice from the whirlwind an answer to Job's question? Why does Job recant or repent in the end? Having heard the Voice from the whirlwind, what does he mean by the statement, "Now my eye sees you"?

However these questions are treated, the poet brings us to an awareness of the great gulf that is fixed between the Creator and the creature. God's wisdom, which grasps the entire scheme of creation, is inaccessible to human beings; God's power that upholds the creation is overwhelming. Perhaps the Book of Job will provide a context for appreciating the message announced at the beginning of the Gospel of John: that the chasm has been bridged, for the Logos (Word) of creation has become flesh (John 1).

Questions to Think About

1. The first psalm suggests that the person who obeys the will of God will enjoy security, prosperity, and long life. Discuss the difference between the attitude of this psalm and that of Psalm 73, with its great "nevertheless" in verse 23.

2. What strengths and weaknesses do you see in Ezra's great reform? Discuss what "legalism" means in the church today.

3. The great keynote of Israel's sages was that "the fear of the Lord is the beginning of wisdom" (Prov 9:10; 15:33; Job 28:28; Ps 111:10). Consider what this means, perhaps by studying the magnificent poem in Job 28.

4. In the satiric *J.B.: A Play in Verse* (Boston: Houghton Mifflin, 1989), Archibald MacLeish probes the meaning of suffering from a modern perspective. What aspects of the poem of Job does he ignore? What new dimensions are added?

5. The test of any religion is how it deals with the problem of suffering and evil. How is this problem dealt with in the prophecy represented by Jeremiah? In Second Isaiah's portrayal of the Suffering Servant? In the Book of Job?

Suggestions for Further Reading

Anderson, Bernhard W. *Contours of Old Testament Theology.* Minneapolis: Fortress Press, 1999. Part III-A, "From Torah to Wisdom."

————. *Understanding the Old Testament.* 5th ed. (with S. Bishop and J. Newman). Upper Saddle River, N.J.: Pearson Prentice Hall, 2006. See chapter 15, "A Kingdom of Priests," chapter 16, "The Praises of Israel," and chapter 17, "The Beginning of Wisdom."

Clines, David J. A. *Ezra, Nehemiah, Esther.* New Century Bible Commentary. Grand Rapids, Mich.: Eerdmans, 1984.

Kidner, D. *Ezra and Nehemiah: An Introduction and Commentary.* Tyndale Old Testament Commentaries. London: InterVarsity, 1979.

Ezra/Nehemiah

Blenkinsopp, Joseph. *Ezra-Nehemiah.* Philadelphia: Westminster John Knox, 1988.

Smith-Christopher, Daniel L. *A Biblical Theology of Exile.* Overtures to Biblical Theology. Minneapolis: Fortress Press, 2002.

Wisdom Literature

Crenshaw, James L. *Old Testament Wisdom: An Introduction.* Atlanta: John Knox, 1981.

Habel, Norman. *The Book of Job.* Old Testament Library. Philadelphia: Westminster, 1985. One of the best commentaries available.

O'Connor, Kathleen M. *The Wisdom Literature.* Wilmington, Del.: Michael Glazier, 1993. Explores the spirituality of Wisdom literature as a resource for contemporary faith.

Rad, Gerhard von. *Wisdom in Israel.* Nashville: Abingdon, 1973.

Scott, R. B. Y. *The Way of Wisdom in the Old Testament.* New York: Macmillan, 1971.

Terrien, Samuel. *Job: Poet of Existence.* Indianapolis: Bobbs-Merrill, 1958.

The Book of Psalms

Anderson, Bernhard W. *Out of the Depths: The Psalms Speak for Us Today.* 3rd ed. (with S. Bishop). Louisville: Westminster John Knox, 2000.

Brueggemann, Walter. *The Message of the Psalms.* Minneapolis: Augsburg Publishing House, 1984.

Eaton, John H. *The Circle of Creation.* London: SCM, 1995.

Gillingham, Susan E. *The Poems and Psalms of the Hebrew Bible.* Oxford: Oxford University Press, 1994.

Mays, James Luther. *Psalms.* Louisville: Westminster John Knox, 1994.

Victory through Defeat

Study Passages

1. Acts 10:34-43
   To Him the Prophets Bear Witness
2. Mark 8:27–9:13
   Peter's Confession
3. 1 Corinthians 1:17–2:9
   The Scandal of the Cross
4. 2 Corinthians 5:14–6:2
   The New Creation

The historical drama, in which God is the Chief Actor, has now reached its climax. The New Testament opens with the exuberant announcement that God's promises to Israel are being fulfilled. John the Baptist, the last of Israel's prophets before the dawn of the messianic age, appears on the scene in a manner reminiscent of Elijah, announcing that the great consummation (the day of judgment and renewal) is at hand. Jesus of Nazareth steps onto the stage of history at this crucial juncture, and his message is pitched to a key of urgency:

> The time is fulfilled, and the kingdom of God is at hand; repent, and believe in the gospel. (Mark 1:15)

THE CHRISTIAN GOOD NEWS

Earlier we saw (in STUDY IV) that the Christian term *gospel* has its scriptural background in passages of Second Isaiah where the prophet, like a herald, announced the good news of God's

coming in triumph to inaugurate a new age (Isa 52:7-10). Likewise, in the New Testament the gospel is the good news of the
dawn of a new age—the beginning of God's redemptive rule.
The good news is not a new doctrine, such as the "fatherhood of
God" (compare Mal 2:10), but is the announcement of what God
does: God delivers humanity from the bondage of evil, darkness, and death, and re-creates human life with new possibilities
of freedom and fulfillment. Moreover, the New Testament proclaims that the good news is Jesus himself—his words and works,
which confront people with the authority of one who is uniquely
anointed to be God's agent. (The Greek word for Christ [*christos*]
is equivalent to the Hebrew word for Messiah [*mashiach*], which
means "anointed one"—that is, one who is consecrated as the
agent of God's rule.)

Jesus preaches with eschatological urgency: *now* is the time
to decide, tomorrow may be too late; for the rule of God is at
hand! (The word "eschatological" comes from the Greek word
eschata, referring to the "last things" or "the end." In this context,
"end" refers to the great consummation, which is so near that it
is already beginning to break into history.) Above all, the gospel
focuses on the crucifixion and, on the other side of this event,
the resurrection. If the exodus was a mighty act of God, if the
deliverance of Jewish exiles from captivity was a divine deed,
then God's greatest miracle in history was what has been called
the "Christ Event"—the whole life, death, and resurrection of
Jesus, and the consequent emergence of the church.

The written Gospels (Matthew, Mark, Luke, John) are not
biographies in our sense of the word but are primarily confessions of faith, each with a different accent and perspective. This
does not mean that the literary Gospels belong in the category
of fiction or fantasy, for the gospel story is based securely on the
earthly career of a historical person. Nevertheless, Jesus' words
and works were remembered in the experience of those who,
after the crucifixion and resurrection, were convinced that he
was God's Messiah (Christ)—the anointed one of God (Acts
10:38). Thus in the earliest Gospel, Mark, the focus of interest

is chiefly on the passion of Christ. Another formulation of the Christian gospel is found in Peter's sermon as presented in Acts 10:34-43, a passage that you should take time to read, for it presents the basic outline of the Christian story.

THE DENOUEMENT
OF THE HISTORICAL DRAMA

To appreciate the Christian conviction that the Christ Event is the fulfillment and climax of the previous episodes of the biblical drama, let's take a brief glance back at what has unfolded thus far. The biblical drama begins by describing in pictorial terms humanity's estrangement from God—the misuse of the freedom God has given and the resulting confusion, conflict, and chaos in history. To deal with this general human predicament, God took the initiative—so we are told in Gen 12:1-3—and called Abraham, promising him that he and his descendants would be a blessing to the broken and distraught families of humankind. So Israel was called and formed as a special community in order that this people might be the bearer of God's purpose in history, the agent for the accomplishment of God's historical plan.

Israel's record, however, was one of persistent betrayal of the covenant loyalty, and the catastrophes that struck in the periods of Assyrian and Babylonian world rule were interpreted by prophets as the discipline of God's judgment. Then, buoyed by the stirring prophecy of Second Isaiah and the leadership of Ezra and Nehemiah, a fresh start was made after the Exile. But in the period of Judaism, Israel became so preoccupied with the problem of preserving its own identity and tradition that the world mission described by Second Isaiah was almost lost to sight, except for a few witnesses like the Book of Jonah. At last, in the fullness of time (Gal 4:4), Jesus of Nazareth appeared in the context of the history of God's people. In the words of a poet:

Then came, at a predetermined moment, a moment in time
and of time,

A moment not out of time, but in time, in what we call history; transecting, bisecting the world of time, a moment in time but not like a moment of time,

A moment in time but time was made through that moment; for without the meaning there is no time, and that moment of time gave the meaning.

T. S. Eliot, *"Choruses from 'the Rock'" VII*[1]

The Christian church affirms that in this "moment of time," which divides history into BCE and CE, God has made a new beginning, an age in which people may begin to experience a richer and fuller humanity. Through Christ, the church proclaims, a new life is available: a new relationship to God and, as a corollary, a new relationship among human beings. Jeremiah's prophecy of the new covenant (see STUDY III) took on deeper meaning for Christians who appropriated the scriptural tradition. The Christian community, like the monastic community that flourished at Qumran on the shore of the Dead Sea,[2] understood itself to be the community of the new covenant. When the shadow of the cross fell upon the table at the Last Supper, Jesus said to his disciples, "This cup is the new covenant in my blood" (1 Cor 11:25; compare Luke 22:20), recalling both the ceremony at Sinai (Exod 24:3-8) and Jeremiah's prophecy (Jer 31:31-34).

THE NEW CHRISTIAN LANGUAGE

The Christian community, however, did not merely repeat the tradition of the past but used it creatively to declare what God is doing now. Perhaps the major characteristic of this community was the new language that it used to tell the Christian gospel. The "narrative mode," Amos Wilder points out, "is uniquely important to Christianity"—unlike other religions and philosophies, in which the telling of a story is relatively peripheral. Like any good drama, the Christian story has a powerful quality that involves its hearers, questions their existence, and draws them into the narrative. In the story of Christ's passion, for example, there are many episodes involving everyday persons, such as the maid in the courtyard of the high priest (Mark 14:66-70) and Simon of Cyrene, who was compelled to bear the cross of Jesus (Mark 15:21). Rather than permitting us to stand at a distance, these minor anecdotes make the Christian story one with which we can identify. As Wilder observes:

> Perhaps the special character of the stories of the New Testament lies in the fact that they are not told for themselves, that they are not only about other people, but they are always about us. They locate us in the very midst of the great story and plot of all time and space, and therefore relate us to the great dramatist and storyteller, God.[3]

WHO DO YOU SAY THAT I AM?

Within this dramatic context, we should read the story of Peter's confession at Caesarea-Philippi and its sequel, the story of the transfiguration (Mark 8:27—9:13). Since this is the turning point in Mark's passion story, the best preparation would be to read the whole Gospel through, sensitive to the role of minor characters in the drama. The recurring question is: Who is this Stranger who speaks with authority, who performs the deeds that evidence God's active presence in the world, who is rejected by the religious authorities and misunderstood by his own followers, and who finally goes his lonely way to the cross? "Who do you say that I am?" Neutrality is out of the question; decision is demanded.

Notice that the mystery of Jesus' identity was heightened by his announcement to his disciples that his vocation was that of the Suffering Servant and that those who follow after him would share his suffering. Strangely, he *must* suffer (Mark 8:31-33). Why this divine necessity? In those days it was generally believed that the Messiah would come triumphantly to restore the lost fortunes of Israel, either by political action or by supernatural power, and achieve thereby a victory that would be clear to all.

How incredible that Second Isaiah's portrayal of the Suffering Servant, which the prophet apparently applied to the sufferings of Israel (see STUDY IV), could be a depiction of the role of the triumphant Messiah!

The story of the transfiguration (Mark 9:2-13) connects the Crucifixion-Resurrection with the previous episodes of the biblical drama. In Israelite tradition, the appearance of a prophet "like Moses" (Deut 18:15-16) or another Elijah (Mal 4:5) would mark the time of the end, the coming of a new age under the redemptive rule of God. It is significant, then, that in the disciples' vision these two figures, Moses and Elijah, appear in company with Jesus. In a kind of religious ecstasy, the disciples perceive the splendid uniqueness of Jesus; but the sequel of Mark's story shows that they could not really understand the divine victory that lay on the other side of the cross. Their continuing lack of faith is a commentary on Jesus' rebuke to Peter for being not on the side of God but on the side of human beings (Mark 8:33).

THE SCANDAL OF THE CROSS

The theme of the mystery of the cross is treated at greater length in a letter Paul addressed to the church at the Greek city of Corinth (1 Cor 1:17—2:13). Here Paul points out that to the nonbeliever, whether Jew or Gentile, the cross is either foolishness or an offense, a stumbling block (skandalon). If the Christian gospel were only the preaching of a loftier ethic or the belief in a supreme being, the world would have little difficulty with this faith. But the trouble is that Christians proclaim the wisdom of God in what the world considers foolishness and the power of God in what the world regards as weakness and defeat. Take away the cross, Paul testifies, and there is no gospel to proclaim. The cross is the distinctive Christian symbol of God's victory in apparent defeat.

Some may think it strange that we do not focus our attention first on Jesus' teachings as found in the Sermon on the Mount (Matthew 5–7). The reason for this is that the early Christians did not start there. *They began, rather, with a recital of the story of Jesus—his passion and his resurrection.* Teachings and ethical exhortations had their proper place after one was drawn into the believing community. The good news was not an ethical code or a new religious idea. It was, rather, the telling of the marvelous story that in Jesus of Nazareth, God had actively entered into the human struggle, changing Jesus' suffering and defeat into victory by raising him from the dead and inaugurating a "new creation." Paul discusses the momentous results of God's action in another communication to the church at Corinth that deserves careful study (2 Cor 5:14—6:2). There he announces the triumphant theme that "God was in Christ reconciling the world" to God's self (2 Cor 5:19)—overcoming the sin that finds expression in our separation from God, from one another, and from our true selves, and restoring us to the unity and dignity that God intends for the creation.

Questions to Think About

1. The custom of dividing the Western calendar into "BC" ("Before Christ") and "AD" ("Anno Domini," or "year of our Lord") goes back to the sixth century, when a monk named Dionysius Exiguus attempted to calculate the date of the birth of Christ. In this book, we use the more neutral designations BCE (Before the Common Era) and CE (Common Era). What is at stake in this discussion about the calendar?

2. Viewed in the light of the New Testament, how is Jesus' death different from the martyrdom of Socrates, Abraham Lincoln, Mohandas Gandhi, or Martin Luther King Jr.? Why was the cross "necessary" to the accomplishment of God's purpose for humankind?

3. Evaluate the popular view that the essence of Christianity is the Golden Rule or the Sermon on the Mount. What is the "new" that has been introduced through God's action in Jesus Christ?

4. The historian Arnold Toynbee once said that the Transfiguration is the key to the Christian interpretation of history. Would you agree?

5. Why might the cross of Jesus be a "scandal" (offense, stumbling block) to people today? Have you become familiar with this "scandalous cross," or are you more familiar with a watered-down Christianity? Discuss the "costs" of Christian discipleship.

Suggestions for Further Reading

Achtemeier, Paul J. *Mark.* Proclamation Commentaries. 2nd rev. ed. Philadelphia: Fortress Press, 1986.

Johnson, Luke T. *The Writings of the New Testament: An Interpretation.* 2nd rev. and enlarged ed. Minneapolis: Fortress Press, 1999.

Kee, Howard. *The Community of the New Age: Studies in Mark's Gospel.* Philadelphia: Westminster, 1977. An illuminating treatment of Mark's Gospel in the light of apocalyptic tradition.

Minear, Paul. *The Gospel according to Mark.* Layman's Bible Commentaries. Richmond: John Knox, 1962. Clear, concise introduction.

Perrin, Norman. *The New Testament: An Introduction.* 2nd ed. Revised by D. Daling. New York: Harcourt Brace Jovanovich, 1982. See chapter 8.

Sanders, E. P. *Jesus and Judaism.* Minneapolis: Fortress Press, 1985.

Wilder, Amos. *The Language of the Gospel.* New York: Harper and Row, 1964. A clearly written, incisive contribution to the understanding of the New Testament.

Wright, N. T. *The Challenge of Jesus: Rediscovering Who Jesus Was and Is.* Downers Grove, Ill.: InterVarsity, 1999.

———. *Jesus and the Victory of God.* Minneapolis: Fortress Press, 1996. An illuminating discussion of Jesus and the apocalyptic tradition by an important Anglican scholar.

The Church in the World

Study Passages

1. Romans 9–11
   The Israel of God
2. 1 Peter 2:4-10
   The Rejected Stone as the Cornerstone
3. Ephesians 1:3 – 2:22
   The Church in God's Universal Design
4. John 17
   That They May Be One

In this study, our attention focuses on a new emergent in history: the church of Jesus Christ. From the very first, Christianity was characterized by an esprit de corps, a sense of membership in a corporate reality that Paul called the body of Christ (1 Cor 12:27). The individualism that characterizes some modern expressions of Christianity is completely foreign to the New Testament, so much so that the phrase "individual Christian" is a contradiction in terms. The various churches at Antioch, Jerusalem, Ephesus, Corinth, and elsewhere were local manifestations of the corporate whole, the body. Jesus himself conceived his mission to be that of calling the remnant of Israel—twelve disciples, corresponding to the twelve-tribe structure of Israel. And when the meaning of Jesus' life, death, and resurrection came upon these disciples with overwhelming power at the festival of Pentecost (Acts 2), one of the major annual festivals of the Israelite calendar, a great miracle occurred. This small community became a dynamic and militant church, with a message that "turned the world upside down" (Acts 17:6) and a gospel that was carried enthusiastically to the ends of the earth. The Acts of the Apostles gives the story of the emerging, expanding church. And every line of the New Testament presupposes the new community.

THE ISRAEL OF GOD

While stressing the newness of the church, we must also keep in mind the relation of this community to the whole Old Testament heritage. In a certain sense, the church may be called the "New Israel." The Old Testament narrates how a people was formed to be the bearer of God's purpose in history and the instrument of God's saving work. Israel was not a race or a nation but a covenant community created by God's action (Exod 15:16b; Ps 100:3; Isa 43:15; 44:2). Having delivered Israel from the miserable lot of slavery in Egypt, God made them a covenant people. Through many tumultuous years, God educated and disciplined them in order that they might understand more deeply the meaning of their special role in history.

It was Second Isaiah who understood most profoundly Israel's place in God's worldwide purpose. According to this prophet, Israel was called to be a "light to the nations" and a servant whose sufferings would benefit all humankind. However, in the period of Judaism, as we have seen, these spacious horizons were obscured. Jewish devotion to the Torah had the effect of sharpening the division between Jew and non-Jew and even separated Jews from their close relatives, the Samaritans (see John 4:7-30, especially verse 9: "For Jews have no dealings with Samaritans"). The last two centuries before Christ witnessed a resurgence of Jewish nationalism that led in time to the Jewish wars with Rome. This story is told in part in 1 Maccabees—a book that belongs to the Old Testament in expanded form (Apocrypha). In 70 CE, under the emperor Titus, the Romans destroyed the Temple, leveled Jerusalem, and removed the last vestiges of Jewish statehood, as depicted on the Arch of Titus in Rome today.

So, in the fullness of time, God acted once again to reconstitute the community of Israel—no longer bound by the ethnic or nationalistic limitations of Judaism but open to all people, whether Jew or Gentile, on the basis of faith. The new community does not establish a clean break with the people of God whose life story is portrayed in the Old Testament. Rather, as Paul puts it in his important discussion in Romans 9–11, the community is a "remnant chosen by grace." It is, so to speak, a "wild olive shoot" grafted onto the olive tree (Israel); and the "branch" is supported by the roots that reach down deeply into the biblical story of God's choice of Israel and God's faithful dealings with this people (Rom 11:17-24). The whole passage deserves thoughtful study, for it casts light upon the affinity between the Jewish and Christian communities, which cannot be effaced by differences over the identity of the Messiah.

THE CORNERSTONE OF THE FOUNDATION

Of the many passages in the New Testament that deal with the calling and mission of the new community, three have been selected for special study. You will find that each deals with an important characteristic of the church. The first of these (1 Pet 2:4-10) brings the accent down upon the truth that this "pilgrim people" has been established by God's action through Jesus Christ, the "living stone," who is the foundation of a "spiritual house." The church is not essentially a social organization or a human institution that can be understood by sociological analysis; it is, rather, a creation of the Divine Architect who has chosen the rejected Stone (Jesus Christ) as the foundation. This imagery harks back to a passage in Psalm 118, a royal thanksgiving that celebrates God's gracious acts in history.[1] In this psalm—Martin Luther's favorite—the key passage is verses 21-24, especially the jubilant cry that the stone which the builders would have rejected as poor material has become the cornerstone of the foundation (compare Isa 28:16). The stone referred to is the remnant of Israel—a "well-tested stone" upon which God would build. According to our passage in 1 Peter, the remnant is reduced to one—to Jesus Christ, the foundation of the church. Notice that the expressions in verse 9 previously had been applied to the chosen people at the time of the making of the covenant (see Exod 19:4-6); now they are applied to the New Israel, which was once "no people" (compare Hos 2:23) but which in the grace of God has become "God's people":

> But you are a chosen race, a royal priesthood, a holy nation, God's own people, that you may declare the wonderful deeds of him who called you out of darkness into his marvelous light. Once you were no people but now you are God's people; once you had not received mercy but now you have received mercy. (1 Pet 2:9-10)

THE CHURCH IN GOD'S WORLD PURPOSE

The place of the church in the movement of God's purpose for the world, from creation to consummation, is developed with symphonic splendor in the Epistle to the Ephesians (Eph 1:1-14; 3:8-12). This epistle is such an eloquent summary of the Christian gospel in Pauline terms that it would be profitable to take a few minutes to read it through.[2] Notice that the church is described in terms of two main images: first, the image of the temple of which Jesus Christ is the chief cornerstone (2:19-22), and second, the distinctively Pauline image of the body of which the head is Christ who coordinates all the parts (1:22-23; 4:15-16; compare Col 1:18-19).

Perhaps it would be helpful to concentrate attention on chapter 2 of Ephesians, where the fundamental theme of the new life and harmonious unity of the church is sounded, a theme that is elaborated in the second part of the epistle (chapters 4–6). Here it is appropriate to look into the biblical meaning of the word "peace" (Greek: *eirēnē;* Hebrew: *shalom*). We usually think of peace as the absence of war, but in the Bible "peace" has a more positive meaning. Peace is a state of harmony, wholeness, and welfare within the community. And it is a basic biblical premise that there cannot be right relations within the community unless human beings are in right relation with God, for, when separated from God, people are at odds with themselves and with one another. The Jewish philosopher Martin Buber has observed:

> The true community does not arise through people's having feelings for one another (though indeed not without it), but through, first, their taking their stand in living mutual relation with the living Centre, and second, their being in living mutual relation with one another.[3]

Thus the commandment about loving God comes first and supplies the basis for loving the neighbor (Luke 10:25-37).

As Old Testament prophets looked away from the fractured society of Israel, they anticipated the coming of the age of the Messiah, when the barriers of separation would be overcome and human beings would be brought into a new relation with God and hence with one another and even with the natural environment (Isa 11:1-9). In Ephesians, love is not a commandment but a new reality in human relationships that has been initiated by the prior manifestation of God's love through Jesus Christ. The most deep-seated antagonism of the time—the separating wall between Jew and Gentile—has been broken down and human beings are reconciled "in one body through the cross." The church is a fellowship of love—the highest endowment of God's Spirit (see 1 Corinthians 13; 1 John 4:7-12).

JESUS' PRAYER FOR THE CHURCH

The theme of the unity and fruitfulness of the church in the world is elaborated in Jesus' so-called high-priestly prayer, in John 17. Jesus has completed his mission, which is to reveal God's "name" (see STUDY 11) to his disciples, the nucleus of the church. In his final prayer, two prepositions are important: "out of" and "into." God has summoned a people for Christ "out of" the world (verse 6). Indeed, the New Testament word for church (*ekklēsia*) literally means "called out" and suggests the idea of

God calling people out of the world into a new and unique fellowship. But the church is not taken out of the world—the secular sphere—into a sheltered and detached life; rather, it is sent "into" the world (verses 15, 18). If the church is not *a part of* the world, it is also not *apart from* the world. Rather, it is God's task force, God's mission in the world. The church has inherited the vocation of the Servant described by Second Isaiah: to be a light to the nations and to be the instrument of God's healing of the broken relationships of society.

Above all, Jesus' prayer is for the unity of the church—"that they may be one, even as we are one" (verses 11, 22). The close relation between Christ and God in the Spirit is to be manifest in the corporate unity and harmony of the church. And this unity is to be the most convincing demonstration to the world that Jesus has been sent by God as the Way, the Truth, and the Life.

Questions to Think About

1. How does Paul deal with the "mystery of Israel" in Romans 9–11? What implication does this passage have for Jewish-Christian relations today?

2. In the Bible, the church is described by various images: flock, vine, building, pilgrim people, body, and so on. What is the intention of each of these images, and how do you respond? Which is most meaningful for our time?

3. Does the breaking down of the "wall of separation" between Jew and Gentile have any implications for other racial and social problems facing the church today? What "wall of separation" might exist between Christians and Muslims? Between Jews and Muslims?

4. What is the relation between the church and the many "churches" of our time? What is the "holy catholic church" of the Apostles' Creed? Does the unity of the church lie in organization? If not, what is the basis of the unity expressed in the words of the familiar hymn, "Elect from every nation, yet one o'er all the earth"?

5. What does it mean in our time for the church to be a mission in the world? What should the Christian's attitude be toward secular expression in art, literature, movies, popular music, social action, and so on?

Suggestions for Further Reading

Barrett, C. K. *A Commentary on the Epistle to the Romans.* Harper's New Testament Commentaries. New York: Harper, 1957. An excellent commentary on Paul's most important letter.

————. *Reading through Romans.* London: SCM, 1977. A more popular yet discerning treatment.

Beker, J. Christiaan. *Paul's Apocalyptic Gospel: The Coming Triumph of God.* Philadelphia: Fortress Press, 1982.

————. *Suffering and Hope: The Biblical Vision and the Human Predicament.* Philadelphia: Fortress Press, 1987.

Minear, Paul. *Images of the Church in the New Testament.* Philadelphia: Westminster, 1960. Especially helpful for this study unit.

Sanders, James A. "Torah and Christ." In *From Sacred Story to Sacred Text.* Philadelphia: Fortress Press, 1987, 41–60. Reprinted from *Interpretation* 29 (1973): 372–90. An illuminating treatment of Christ as "God's climactic act" in the biblical story.

Segal, Alan F. *Paul the Convert: The Apostolate and Apostasy of Saul the Pharisee.* New Haven: Yale University Press, 1990. An illuminating study of Paul's Jewish convictions as they challenged and influenced his conversion to faith in Jesus.

Epilogue: In the End

Study Passages

1. Revelation 21:1-8 and 21:22—22:5
   A New Heaven and a New Earth
   The New Jerusalem
2. 1 Corinthians 15 (especially 15:12-23, 51-58)
   The Resurrection of the Body
3. Romans 8:18-39
   More Than Conquerors
4. 1 Thessalonians 4:13-18
   The Triumphant Return

Like any drama, the biblical drama has a beginning, a climax or denouement, and an end. This elementary observation is exceedingly important for the understanding of the biblical view of history. Unlike the ancient Greek historians who believed that history moves in circles, and unlike some modern historians who believe that the historical process is a phase of the growth and decay of nature, the Bible affirms that our lives are part of a great drama that moves in the direction of a goal. The opening words of the Bible, "In the beginning God . . . ," are matched by the expectation that "in the end" God's purpose will be realized (1 Cor 15:24-28). All things—history and nature, heaven and earth—are caught up in the purpose of the God who is the First and the Last, the Alpha and the Omega. Therefore, telling the time is not just a chronological reckoning by clocks and calendars; it is the ability to know the content of the times (Ecclesiastes 3) and to discern that, as a psalmist put it, our times are in God's hand (Ps 31:15), embraced within the divine sovereign purpose.

THE HORIZONS OF HISTORY

It has been observed that when it comes to the interpretation of human history there are, in general, three possible views: (1) history is meaningless flux from which the religious person seeks escape (Hinduism, Buddhism); (2) history secretes its own meaning in the course of cultural evolution (Progress, Marxism); and (3) the hidden meaning of history is made known by God who, as Creator, transcends the whole finite world of sensory experience. The biblical view is that the meaning of the historical drama has its source in the Creator who comprehends the beginning and the end, who surveys and participates in the drama in its entirety, and who, according to Christian conviction, has set forth the mystery of God's will in Jesus Christ as a "plan" that unites all things, earthly and cosmic (Eph 1:9-10).

In the first study unit, we considered the prologue to the biblical drama of God's action in history. Now we turn our attention to the epilogue. It should be obvious that we cannot speak of either the first things or the last things except in the language of religious symbolism. In both cases we are dealing with ultimates that lie beyond the range of our finite knowledge, beyond our immediate historical experience. Therefore we must speak in the language of faith—faith that rests not upon our ability to fathom or to chart the beginning and the end but upon the meaning that has been disclosed in the unique historical tradition beginning with the exodus and culminating in the Christ event. In the vision of Christian faith, human history as we know it is bounded by Beginning and End, two horizons that recede into the vistas of God's eternity.

PARADISE REGAINED

A good place to begin the discussion is with the portrayal of the new heaven and the new earth found in the last book of the New Testament, the Revelation (or Apocalypse) of Saint John the Divine. This is an exceedingly difficult book to understand because it is written in a code that cannot be deciphered without some knowledge of the persecution of the church at the time (about 90 CE) and the genre of literature known as "apocalyptic."[1] Much confusion has been wrought by people who have read the book as though they were gazing into a crystal ball, supposing that some mysterious blueprint for the future is hidden in it. I have tried to facilitate the study by selecting two brief passages (Rev 21:1-8; 21:22—22:5) in which the symbolism is not quite so obtuse. Even so, there are references that will not mean much without the help of a good commentary. For instance, "The Sea was no more" (21:1) is an allusion to the mythical Great Deep, the locus of rebellious powers that God has held in check since the time of Creation.[2] In other words, this is not the drying-up of water but the overcoming of the powers of evil that menace God's creation. (Herman Melville's novel *Moby Dick* makes effective use of the biblical sea symbolism.) And the Lamb, of course, is the triumphant Christ (see John 1:29).

Two things are especially noteworthy about these passages. First, the portrayal of the new heaven and the new earth (compare Isa 65:17-25) gathers up some of the symbols of the paradise story, such as the tree of life. Thus the end of the biblical drama recapitulates the beginning: the new creation corresponds to the first creation. Second, the consummation of history is symbolized under the figure of the New Jerusalem, the city of God, descending from heaven. In previous studies we have found that Jerusalem in biblical tradition was more than an ordinary city. Jerusalem meant much more to the Israelite than Athens to an ancient Greek or Washington, D.C., to a present-day American. According to the "urban theology" developed in Davidic circles, Jerusalem was the city of God, the place consecrated by God's presence among the people. Indeed, Jerusalem was identified with the mythical mountain of God at the center ("navel") of the earth, from which sprang a river fed by life-giving waters from the great deep (Ps 46:4; Ezek 47:1-12). Medieval maps that pinpointed Jerusalem as the center of the universe were based on bad geography and astronomy. But they expressed an important religious conviction.

In the perspective of Christian faith, Jerusalem stands for the rule of God in the center of the world, as in Augustine's classical work *The City of God* or in Haydn's hymn "Glorious things of thee are spoken, Zion, city of our God." In the Apocalypse of John, the bold claim is made that history ultimately will fulfill and complete the meaning represented by Jerusalem: all nations will find their peace and unity by walking in the light of the new Jerusalem (Rev 21:24-26; compare Isa 2:1-4).

Thus the Bible begins with a vision of paradise lost and concludes with a vision of paradise regained. In between this prologue and this epilogue unfolds the drama of God's entrance into the human struggle to win back the lost creation and to restore humanity to peace, unity, and fullness of life. God's strategy involves the choice and discipline of a people—and finally the way of the cross. But the end of God's redemptive activity is the final conquest of evil, death, darkness, and all powers that corrupt and threaten the creation. The church lives by this hope and prays and strives for the coming of God's divine realm.

THE DECISIVE BATTLE IS WON!

This brings us to the third passage, a portion of 1 Corinthians 15. The background of this passage is the apocalyptic view, expressed in Dan 12:2-3 and Isa 26:19, of the final consummation (the Last Judgment), when the dead will be raised up in order that the faithful may share in the conclusion of the historical drama.[3] In much of the chapter, Paul argues that the "body" that will be raised is not the physical body but a *spiritual* body, surpassing the present form of our bodily existence. It is worth noting, in passing, that the body is considered to be the expression of the *person* in the wholeness of the person's personality, the unique self who finds life in relation to other persons and to God.[4] Don't stumble over the literal details. Paul's intention is to affirm that the individual is *given* a future by the God who is gracious and faithful, although exactly how this is to occur, says Paul, is "a mystery" (1 Cor 15:51).

The important thing to notice in this passage is that God's victory over evil, darkness, and death has already occurred—even before the end, which is described pictorially in the Revelation of John as "a new heaven and a new earth." Of this, the Christian has already been given assurance through the resurrection of Christ, for his victory constitutes the "first fruits" that give promise that the harvest is coming (1 Cor 15:20). Or, as Paul puts it elsewhere, through Christ's resurrection we have been given the Spirit as an "earnest" or guarantee of what is to come (2 Cor 1:22; 5:5).

This means that the center of gravity in the Christian gospel is not a longing for a consummation yet to come. The distinctive note of the New Testament is the announcement that the Messiah, the Christ, has already come to inaugurate God's redemptive rule. Already Christ has won the decisive victory, and therefore through him humanity may taste now the life of the new age, "eternal life." A New Testament scholar, Oscar Cullmann, has expressed the relationship between the "already" and the "not yet" in a figure of speech drawn from political experience. In some wars of the past, the decisive battle occurred at an early stage of the campaign (for instance, the Battle of Britain during the Second World War). Although the struggle continued until the end of the war, the issue had already been decided. Cullmann uses this as an analogy to express the Christian conviction that the "earnest" or "down payment" of God's ultimate triumph has been given in the life, death, and resurrection of Jesus Christ, even though the historical struggle continues for an indefinite time until the outcome is evident to all.[5] In other words, the Christian gospel is a call to action in a contest whose final victory has *already* been won. Members of the Christian community who share this conviction live in the hope that ultimately God's rule will be fulfilled and that "God will be everything to everyone" (1 Cor 15:28).

It is significant, then, that Paul ends his discussion of the body of the resurrection not with speculation about the life beyond the grave but with an appeal for action and responsibility (note the "therefore" of 1 Cor 15:58). There is a profound this-worldliness in the New Testament gospel, especially when it is read in the context of the whole biblical drama. The ultimate horizon of the consummation, when all tears will be wiped away and there will be no more mourning or suffering, is intended as an endorsement of the fundamental goodness of life as we now experience it. The Christian gospel is not a utopian promise that human beings can achieve the good society through their own planning and efforts; nor is it the promise of release from the changes and transience of mortal existence, as in some Hellenistic cults of the New Testament period. Rather, it announces that none of our work is in vain because it is embraced within the purpose and love of God manifested in the midst of human history through Jesus Christ.

This is the theme to which Paul returns in the last and major letter that he wrote: the epistle to the church at Rome (Rom 8:18-19). Paul looks squarely at the sufferings of the present age, the tremendous odds that are arrayed against the realization of God's purpose. He is more impressed, however, with the victory *already* won and the opportunity to share in the power of that victory in the present. The motive for action and responsibility is the confidence that all our human successes and failures, our joys and sorrows, are embraced within the triumphant purpose of God. "In everything," writes Paul, "God works for good with those who love him" (Rom 8:28). Thus, though the trials and conflicts of history are not yet concluded, the believing community lives in the assurance that "in all these things we are more than conquerors through him who loved us" (Rom 8:37).

THE TRIUMPHANT RETURN
OF JESUS CHRIST

Many people turn to the apocalyptic dimension of the Bible because of a deep foreboding about the end of human life on our planet. The earth, we are told, cannot sustain human life indefinitely, owing to human pollution and industrial corruption. Natural disasters beyond human control, such as tsunamis or volcanic eruptions, are reminders of the widespread devastation that could fall upon us at any moment. Faced with this uncertainty, believers occasionally divest themselves of worldly possessions and gather together in an appointed place to await "the end of the world." These gatherings are often treated with humor in the media and are easily dismissed when life goes on. But this is serious business. Concern for "the last things" (eschatology) is fundamental in Christian belief, at least the faith that is anchored in Scripture and particularly in the New Testament.

From the very first, Christian hope has found its characteristic expression in the announcement that Jesus, the apparently defeated Messiah of God, will return triumphantly to inaugurate God's rule on earth. Initially Jesus' return was described as *parousia*, a Greek word meaning "presence." In the Christian scenario as portrayed at the end of the Gospel of Luke and the beginning of Acts, Jesus has "ascended to heaven," and in this sense is absent from us, but he will return to earth and be present once again as Leader and Savior—as expected in the remembrance of his disciples in the Lord's Supper. Even yet the Eucharist affirms:

> We remember his death,
> We proclaim his resurrection,
> We await his coming in glory.

This hope for Christ's return has fired the zeal of a number of Christians who look for the consummation of history in the "rapture."[6] They are attracted by the words in 1 Thess 4:16-17—one of the earliest expressions of Christian faith in the New Testament—that in the end time Christ himself "with a cry of command, with the archangel's call, and with the sound of the trumpet of God" will descend from heaven. The dead in Christ will rise first, then "we who are alive, who are left, shall be caught up together with them in the clouds" and meet Christ in the air. Notice that Paul's address to the Thessalonians deals with a practical question: What about those who have already died, before the *parousia*? In answer to this question, a distinction is drawn between two kinds of people: (1) those who are "asleep in Christ," that is, in union with Christ after death and awaiting the final resurrection; and (2) those of us who are still alive, who are left behind and ultimately will be raised to be with Christ forever. And the passage ends on a practical note: "Therefore encourage each other with these words."

In this whole discussion we are moving over deep and murky waters. How can we relate the "rapture" and other theological statements to historical reality? Do crucifixion, resurrection, and the second coming stand on the same level? The phrase "crucified under Pontius Pilate" has a ring of historical fact—Jesus was a historical figure and crucifixion was a Roman mode of execution. "Raised on the third day according to the scriptures" is much more difficult but is arguable.[7] "He will come again in glory" is a different kind of statement—it seems to point into the mysterious future of God.

One thing to keep in mind is that this language should not be taken literally but as a symbolic and pictorial expression of faith. In the Gospels of the New Testament, we are given many warnings not to brood or speculate about these things, which are hidden in the wisdom of God. Instead, we are prompted to carry out our tasks of Christian discipleship, serving God by making God's rule on earth a reality in our daily relationships. Notice that in the New Testament Gospels, the accent falls on the power of Christ's resurrection, not on the crucifixion and the violence of those who did away with Jesus. The Gospel of Luke, for example, does not linger on the story of Jesus' death and the agony of the cross but leads into the story of Jesus' real presence in the breaking of bread (Eucharist), displayed powerfully in the story of the walk to Emmaus (Luke 24).

The Christian church is a community of hope, and that hope is expressed in the expectation that Jesus Christ will come again to demonstrate God's triumph over all opposing powers of sin, violence, and death. The Gospels make clear, however, that God's redemptive rule has already come in the life, death, and resurrection of Jesus Christ. Christians believe that Christ's victory embraces all people in all times: those who went before, those now living, and those who come after. In this universal context, we are commissioned to be "ambassadors for Christ" (2 Cor 5:20).

Questions to Think About

1. What dramatic effect is achieved in the Bible by placing the historical drama between the horizons of Beginning and End? Compare this portrayal with other views of human existence, such as the Buddhist, the humanist, the Communist, and the nihilist.

2. Is it proper to identify God's rule on earth with the better world that human beings hope to achieve through social planning or revolutionary action? Is the "kingdom of God" a social ideal?

3. Does it make sense to say that a new age under God's rule has already been inaugurated through the life, death, and resurrection of Jesus Christ, even before the final consummation? Can the second coming (*parousia*) be regarded as more than pictorial language? What changes has the "dawn of a new age" made in human life?

4. How does the Christian's "ultimate hope" affect or motivate one's political and social responsibilities in the present historical order? What are some of the "proximate hopes" that we may expect to realize?

5. Traditionally, Christianity has preferred to express belief in the future life in terms of the resurrection of the body rather than in terms of the dualistic doctrine of the immortality (deathlessness) of the soul. Comment on the difference between these two ways of expression. Why is the former more appropriate for the confession of Christian faith, as in the Apostles' Creed?

Suggestions for Further Reading

Anderson, Bernhard W. *Contours of Old Testament Theology.* Minneapolis: Fortress Press, 1999. See especially Part III-B, "From Prophecy to Apocalyptic."

————. *Understanding the Old Testament.* 5th ed. (with S. Bishop and J. Newman). Upper Saddle River, N.J.: Pearson Prentice Hall, 2006. See chapter 18, "The Unfinished Story."

Caird, G. B. *A Commentary on the Revelation of Saint John the Divine.* Harper's New Testament Commentary. New York: Harper and Row, 1966.

Collins, Adela Yarbro. *Crisis and Catharsis: The Power of the Apocalypse.* Philadelphia: Westminster, 1984.

Faley, R. J. *Apocalypse Then and Now: A Companion to the Book of Revelation.* New York: Paulist, 1999.

Kung, Hans. *On Being a Christian.* New York: Doubleday, 1976, 356–61. A meaningful discussion of the hope of resurrection.

Minear, Paul S. *I Saw a New Earth: An Introduction to the Visions of the Apocalypse.* Washington, D.C.: Corpus Publications, 1968. This book will reward study.

Russell, D. S. *The Method and Message of Jewish Apocalyptic.* Old Testament Library. Philadelphia: Westminster, 1965. A reliable survey of apocalyptic literature from 200 BCE to 100 CE.

Schüssler Fiorenza, Elisabeth. *The Book of Revelation—Justice and Judgment.* 2nd ed. Philadelphia: Fortress Press, 1998.

Suggestions for Bible Study Leaders

PURPOSE

Those who plan to set up a Bible study group should have at the outset some understanding of the uniqueness of the venture. This is not a literary circle devoted to the study of one of the great books. The uniqueness of a Bible study group lies in that which is at the center: the Bible. The Bible continues to exert a strange power over people's lives. It searchingly exposes the human situation in the light of God's Word, spoken in human words and finally made flesh in Jesus Christ. It deals with our human story and God's involvement in it. Since all of us are inescapably involved in human existence with its glory and complexity and tragedy, there should be a place in the group for any concerned person. Those with Christian convictions (and probably they will be in the majority) will find in the Bible a deeper understanding of the relevance of biblical faith to personal life and world history. Skeptics who are sincerely seeking light on the meaning of human existence may discover that in some respects the Bible speaks to their condition. But all members of the group will have a common purpose: to hear what the language of the Bible says to us in our life situation today.

The key word for Bible study is "encounter." What takes place in the group is personal encounter with one another and with the God who speaks to us through the Bible. This distinguishes Bible study from the kind of classroom study in which our primary relation is to a body of knowledge rather than to persons. However, the personal encounter of a Bible study group is not that of a glorified bull session in which discussion is carried on in an argumentative spirit, usually without any common frame of reference. In this case, the conversation has a common center, a common frame of reference. There will be disagreements, for we each approach the Bible out of our private and cultural background, which usually means with a great deal of ignorance and even rebellion. It is the testimony of the ages, however, that God speaks to us as persons when we listen to the language of the Bible receptively, expectantly, honestly. Often this means that the presuppositions of the questions we bring to the Bible are challenged; often it means the realization that we have not asked the basic question; often it means being disturbed and changed at the very center of our being. But this is what we must expect if we risk an encounter with God. The Trappist monk Thomas Merton wisely observes:

> It is of the very nature of the Bible to affront, perplex and astonish the human mind. Hence the reader who opens the Bible must be prepared for disorientation, confusion, incomprehension, perhaps outrage.[1]

LEADERSHIP

Who should be the leader? This is a difficult question. Some groups have effectively used the principle of rotation—that is, at each meeting a different member of the group assumes the leadership role. A possible snag in this approach is that some members might not be far enough along in their understanding of the Bible to lead a discussion (and if the blind lead the blind . . . !) Other groups have found that it is better to rely on a leader who is more mature in biblical understanding (this may be a theological student, a staff leader, a professor, or a minister). No rule of thumb can be given, since groups vary so much.

Qualities of good leadership. The main task of the leader is to help the group go to the heart of the biblical passage, so that there may be a genuine encounter with the Bible rather than a mere rearranging of prejudices. This means that the leader should have some ability in group discussion and should have a fairly good knowledge of the Bible (though not necessarily that of an expert). The good leader is one who brings the discussion back to the biblical passage when the group wanders astray, who patiently guides the discussion so that disagreements are fruitful, who encourages others to participate in the conversation, and who helps the group go deeper than answers that merely scratch the surface and avoid hasty rejection of what some may think they have outgrown. Above all, the leader is the servant of the group and should encourage the rest to have a sense of responsibility for the preparation and participation that will make the study a vital group experience.

Preparation. It cannot be emphasized too strongly that this is a study group in the best sense of the word. Therefore the success of the group is dependent upon disciplined and serious preparation on the part of all members. At the minimum, this preparation must be the careful reading and pondering of the selected biblical passages with the aid of the book. This applies especially to the leader. Careful study of the material will enable the leader to discern what is central and what is peripheral in the group discussion. Also, the leader should be acquainted with the necessary background material for understanding the passages, turning whenever possible for guidance to the "Suggestions for Further Reading" at the ends of the introductory section and each study unit, and at the end of this section. It never hurts to read the text again and again, and in its broader context. A passage in Mark, for instance, may become clearer in the total context of the full Gospel of Mark.

Resource persons. Often study groups include a "resource person" such as a minister, teacher, or staff member who can be consulted when information is needed on a particular point. It is important that such a person be both congenial and modest—not the kind of person who will "lord it over the group." On the other hand, knowledgeable persons might tend to lean over backward on this matter: they are so afraid of dominating the discussion that they do not speak until spoken to. Somehow this should be worked out so that the resource person is truly an active member of the group—on a level of equality with other participants rather than being set up on a pedestal because of a presumed superior knowledge. Perhaps it would be well to forget about the idea of a "resource person" and think rather of team leadership, in which a novice and an experienced person cooperate in preparing for the meeting and guiding the discussion.

PROCEDURE IN THE GROUP SESSION

First of all, help the members of the group to feel at home with one another. In a classroom you can get by without knowing who is sitting next to you, for your concern is the mastery of a body of knowledge, not a relationship between persons. Bible study, however—as we have said—is a relationship with persons by means of the spoken word and an encounter with God whose Word is mediated through human words. Since the Word of God establishes personal relationship rather than communicating a body of facts, the rapport of interpersonal relationship in the group is essential.

At some point in this informal opening the leader should begin the discussion of the selected biblical passage(s). In some situations it might be appropriate to have a brief prayer or a few moments of silence. The important thing, however, is that the entire Bible study be carried on in a serious and reverent spirit.

It should be kept in mind, above all, that Bible study is an interaction between the text and the readers, between the Bible and the situation in which we find ourselves.[2] This premise of group discussion has two interrelated aspects:

1. The primary task is to understand what the biblical writer intended to say. This may involve such questions as, Who was the author? When was the text written? What was the historical and cultural setting? To whom was the writing addressed?
2. Closely related to this is the question about what the text means *for us* in our historical and cultural situation. This calls for an exercise of imagination, like that of actors who

put themselves into the script of a play. Remember that "the letter kills, it is the Spirit that gives life." The Bible should not be treated as a soothsayer's manual that gives us literal, specific directives on everything under the sun. It may be that there are some places in the Bible where, as someone has said, God does not say anything to us except perhaps, "Go, read a commentary!"

Accordingly, the leader may begin by giving whatever brief background is necessary for the study of the selected biblical passage in modern-day language. Perhaps on subsequent occasions the leader could ask other members of the group to do this in order that the group as a whole may sense a shared responsibility. After this brief introduction of the passage, or perhaps before, it would be well to ask the group to read through the passage—or some portion of it—silently. The more group members have read the selected texts ahead of time, the more familiar they will be with the message of the text, and the more rewarding the results of the study session are likely to be. Or it may be decided to ask someone to read the passage, or a small unit of it, aloud. Many of our selected texts have an oral quality to them (the Psalms, for example). If there are difficult words, they should be explained. *It is important to turn to another translation of the passage for additional light.*

Sometimes groups have found it helpful to begin the discussion by attempting to paraphrase the passage in terms of our own modern language—that is, "put it in your own words." This is a good discipline, for it demands (1) coming to terms with what the original writers meant to say, and (2) interpreting their intentions in our own categories. This may occasion the interaction between the Bible and our situation, which, as we have said, is the very essence of Bible study. Moreover, this gets away from the false idea of private interpretation of the Bible. *We do not have the right to make the Bible say what we think it ought to say.* We must discover what the original writer meant to say and translate that meaning into the experiences of our time. Group conversation around the Bible, guided by the Holy Spirit, will lead to a deeper understanding of biblical truth. Don't be afraid to raise "unorthodox" questions, for these may help to sharpen the issues, and God may use the skeptic to lead us into new truth. On the other hand, don't be afraid of "orthodoxy"—only try to "beat the crust back into the batter" of Christian experience. The questions included in the study guide at the end of each unit may help initiate and focus the discussion.

The discussion should move according to blocks of Scripture that the leader has isolated in private preparation. When the leader senses that it is time to move on, a summary of a given unit of material may be given. Above all, the leader should not be anxious about the discussion, as though its success were dependent upon keeping it going. Don't be troubled when there are periods of silence. Don't try to hurry the group along because of the feeling that a given amount of material has to be covered; it is better to stay with a passage until the group is ready to move on. Don't answer important questions too quickly; it may be better to wait patiently for the group to come to the answer on its own. Or perhaps the question should be left open or held over until the next gathering. The leader's purpose is not to lead the group to conclusions foreseen during the preparation; rather, let the conclusion come out of the dialectic of the discussion.

CLOSING THE SESSION

Close on time if possible. The leader may signal the end of the discussion by giving a brief summary and showing the relation of the discussion to the previous study session or to studies that follow. It may be appropriate to follow the summary with a brief prayer, such as the words found in Ps 139:23-24.

Keep in mind that the foregoing remarks are only general suggestions. No plan should be superimposed inflexibly upon a Bible study group.

Suggestions for Further Reading

Orientation

Consult some of my writings, such as "Reading the Bible in the Twenty-First Century" (pp. 99–105 in this volume); and "The Contemporaneity of the Bible," *Princeton Seminary Bulletin* 62 (1969): 38–50.

For a series of explorations in biblical interpretation, see my *The Living Word of the Bible* (Philadelphia: Westminster, 1979). For a theological perspective, see my *Contours of Old Testament Theology* (Minneapolis: Fortress Press, 1999).

Method of Bible Study

For an understanding of the practice of *Lectio Divina* (divine reading), consult *Opening the Bible* by the Trappist monk Thomas Merton (Collegeville, Minn.: Liturgical Press, 2000). The creative teacher will find help from a leader in Bible study such as Hans Rudi Weber, *The Bible Comes Alive: New Approaches for Bible Study Groups* (Valley Forge, Pa.: Judson, 1996); and from the special approach of Walter Wink, *Transforming Bible Study: A Leader's Guide* (Nashville: Abingdon, 1989). Helpful suggestions for leading small Bible study groups are given by Roberta Hestenes in *Using the Bible in Groups* (Philadelphia: Westminster John Knox, 1985).

Commentaries and Guides

In general, the commentaries in the *Old Testament Library* (Philadelphia: Westminster) and the *Interpretation* series (Atlanta: John Knox) are helpful. For a list of useful one-volume commentaries, see the "Suggestions for Further Reading" in the introduction to this guide. An additional resource is the *Collegeville Bible Commentary* on the Old Testament (ed. Robert J. Karris; Collegeville, Minn.: Liturgical Press, 1992). This commentary, with study questions, is written by Roman Catholic scholars especially for general readers, the self-study of the Bible, and adult religious-education programs. William Barclay's classic devotional guide for the New Testament has been reissued as the *New Daily Study Bible* (17 vols.; Philadelphia: Westminster John Knox, 2004). See also the multiauthor Old Testament counterpart, *The Daily Study Bible: Old Testament* (ed. John C. L. Gibson; 24 vols.; Philadelphia: Westminster John Knox, 1987).

Translations

It is important to encourage participants in Bible study to consult more than one translation and even to wonder about differences in translation. Turn to a scholar for help when necessary. The following translations are recommended:

New Revised Standard Version. An ecumenical version in the tradition of the Authorized or King James Version. Highly recommended.

Revised English Bible (rev. ed.; Cambridge: Cambridge University Press, 2002; orig. publ.1989). This complete revision of the *New English Bible* is a lyrical modern translation, widely used in churches throughout the United Kingdom.

New International Version. A beautiful translation by a team of conservative, evangelical scholars.

New Jerusalem Bible. An excellent translation by Roman Catholic scholars under the sponsorship of the L'Ecole Biblique in Jerusalem.

Tanakh. An excellent translation under the auspices of the Jewish Publication Society of America.

New American Bible: With Revised New Testament and Revised Book of Psalms. The official Roman Catholic text for public reading in the United States.

Reading the Bible in the Twenty-First Century

If the legendary Rip Van Winkle had gone to sleep in the early 1950s, when this book was first published, and then awakened today after more than a half century of slumber, he would have been stunned by the new and different world of the present. Many advances in technology have transformed daily life. There is a new global economy that makes all nations interdependent. Christianity and other religions coexist in a pluralistic society. The United States plays a new and fateful role as world leader in the fight against terrorism. In spite of all these changes, however, the Bible continues to hold its outstanding place in world literature. Especially in the translation known as the King James Bible, it is a classic of the English language. Moreover, the ancient Hebrew Bible—known in the Christian community as the Old Testament—is sacred scripture in three major religions: Judaism, Christianity, and Islam.

From this twenty-first-century perspective, there are essentially three ways of reading the Bible. One is to read it as literature, treating it as a literary classic of such high quality that it may be regarded as inspired. This is an appropriate approach, since much of the Bible is cast in poetry and various literary forms that display artistic composition. Another way of reading the Bible is through what is called "historical-critical" study. This approach recognizes that the biblical narratives were written in a historical community and reflect the history and social setting of their times. A third way is to read the Bible as a theological document that expresses the faith and religious struggles of the believing community.

All of these perspectives—literary appreciation, historical study, and biblical theology—are interwoven throughout this book. Our approach to the Bible as "unfolding drama" allows us to take into account the interrelated dimensions of story and history, of early traditions and final literary formulation ("canon"). Further, it invites us to participate in what I have called the "dramatic movement of Scripture."[1] Viewed in this way, "the Bible is not a book to be read but a drama in which to participate."[2] In this sense the unfolding drama can be regarded as "the story of our lives."

THE BIBLE AS HISTORY

Our approach to the Bible as unfolding drama stands firmly in the tradition of "historical criticism," a method of study that takes into account the social and historical background of the biblical narratives as we seek to understand the meaning of the Bible today. This method, while richly rewarding, must be carefully balanced. Some of the material in the Bible is factual and can be accepted as literally true. But it is not adequate simply to read these scriptures as factual history, as some interpreters have tried to do. The biblical record calls for critical study and reflection, taking into account the human dimensions of culture and faith. On the other hand, it would be unwise to surrender to the temptation to go to the opposite extreme, downplaying or even ignoring the related dimension of ordinary history as some interpreters have done (see below).

Keep in mind, however, that this historical method of study should not be seen as a means to recover the past as it "really happened." Biblical archaeology so far has not been able to deliver on its promise to support and validate the biblical record. To take a major example: the fall of Jericho and the swift conquest of the West Bank by invading Israelites, as reported in the book of Joshua, has been contradicted by intensive archaeological investigation. Many have come to doubt whether the biblical record can be relied upon as a historical witness to the events it narrates.

THE POSTMODERNIST VIEW

In particular, the historical witness of the Bible has been challenged by the late-twentieth-century intellectual outlook labeled "postmodernism." The postmodern view is very diverse—perhaps better understood as a cultural atmosphere than a definite movement. Its advocates can be seen as taking their cue from the nineteenth-century philosopher Friedrich Nietzsche (1844–1900), who believed that language is not the medium of reason but of imagination. By means of imagination, according to Nietzsche, we "construct" a world that has nothing to do with the real world or with a metaphysical world that lies beyond our perception. Language has no "referent" beyond itself; it is an imaginative construct.

Consider what this linguistic philosophy means for the study of the Bible. Postmodernists would deny that human speech can ever reach the reality that is beyond language, for instance, a historical event that supposedly happened, or a metaphysical view of God who transcends the world. Accordingly, some postmodernists maintain that there is no intrinsic, stable meaning in a text, but only the meaning that individual interpreters provide. For them, contemporary interpreters are necessarily culturebound, and their social context determines how they construe meaning in a text.

THE BIBLE AS "SALVATION HISTORY"

A predominant way of viewing Scripture has been as *Heilsgeschichte* (German for "history of salvation")—the history of God's redemptive purpose. This view goes back into the New Testament itself (for example, to Luke and, in a profounder sense, to Paul). It was picked up by Irenaeus in the second century and came into its own in a line of theologians extending from Johannes Cocceius in the seventeenth century to Oscar Cullmann and Gerhard von Rad in the twentieth century.

The view of Scripture as *Heilsgeschichte* continues to be meaningful, though some interpreters have questioned its adequacy. Indeed, the "history of salvation" should not be seen as a kind of objective history, manifest in a sequence of events that move inexorably through the Old Testament period to the New. For one thing, the discontinuity between the Old Testament and the New is too deep to allow for any simplistic historical understanding. For another, archaeological and historical research have helped us to realize that God's purpose cannot be traced in a sequence of historical events (a "history" in the ordinary sense) or in a reconstruction of historical events.

Nevertheless, a dramatic reading of the "movement of Scripture"—one that engages the imagination and appeals to the reader or hearer *to be involved in the story*—is rooted in Scripture itself.

THE BIBLE AS OUR STORY

In a profound sense, the Bible presents the story of a "pilgrim people"—to use an expression from the documents of the Second Vatican Council—a people who are summoned to be on the move toward God's future. This story is curiously mixed with the "history" of Israel and the "history" of the early church, showing that it is not divorced from the concrete circumstances of human life in all their tragedy and triumph, in all their sinfulness and faith. The story is not just ancient history, shut up in the dead and unrecoverable past, but a living tradition, an ongoing story in which God continues to speak anew to the people. When the Christian community rereads this story of the pilgrim people, it does so not under the supposition that the story is about someone else, but rather with the understanding that it is "our story"—"the story of our life," as H. Richard Niebuhr has put it.[3]

Moreover, in a larger sense this story is not just a story about the people of God, Israel, and—correlated with it in God's elective purpose—the church. The story is part of a much larger story involving all humanity and all creation—a "cosmic journey" that moves from creation to consummation, from first things to last things. This is the vision that has fired the imagination down through the centuries: the vision of the involvement of all humanity, and indeed of all creatures, in an unfolding drama extending from God's creation to the consummation of God's purpose for the creation.

This view of "dramatic movement" allows us to see that there is unity within the manifest diversity of Scripture, that a dynamic movement or development takes place within the horizons of beginning and end, and that crucial events occur at the climax or denouement that give meaning to the whole. For the Jewish community, what are decisive are the events of the Exodus and Sinai, and the unfolding tradition based on those "root experiences." For the Christian community, the crucial event, which is related in some sense to the Jewish tradition, is the Christ Event—the life, death, and resurrection of Jesus Christ—and the unfolding meaning of this turning point in history.

OUT OF MY LIFE AND THOUGHT

To be sure, we cannot understand the dramatic movement of Scripture just by reading the Bible or going to church. In my own case, the dramatic view of Scripture was presented subtly, indirectly, and, indeed, despite the teaching and liturgy to which I was exposed as a boy. My father, ministering to small frontier congregations in central California, preached a view of Scripture that, by the time I graduated from the College of the Pacific, seemed discouragingly naive—so much so that I almost gave up the faith! Despite this, however, the worshipping community gave me very early in life some sense—inadequate as it was—of the power of the gospel centering in Jesus and his role in the biblical story, and in a mysterious way led me to the ministry.

A decisive moment in my appreciation of the dramatic character of Scripture occurred when I started teaching in the late forties and early fifties and was drawn into the Student Christian Movement—the SCM in the United States—and the larger World Student Christian Federation centered in Geneva, Switzerland. At that time students commonly gathered together in Bible study groups, seeking the opportunity to wrestle with life's purpose and to be drawn closer together in religious understanding. It was students who pressed the theologians with the larger questions of the relation of the parts to the whole, of the episodes to the "unfolding drama of the Bible," in the words of the title of this book, which I wrote in cooperation with students at Bucknell University.

A more recent influence on my understanding of the dramatic movement of Scripture comes from my growing appreciation of "the holy catholic church," to use the language of the Apostles' Creed. The majestic creeds, rich symbolism, and engaging liturgy of worship in the church invite one to participate in a shared experience of the divine drama. As Amos Wilder has observed, the biblical narratives of Scripture "locate us in the very midst of the great story and plot of all time and space." In worship we celebrate our relationship to God, "the great dramatist and storyteller."[4]

A NEW BEGINNING

As we seek to understand the Bible in a new millennium, we have learned some important things from postmodern interpretation. For one thing, what we perceive in the Bible is dependent upon where we stand: the culture in which we have been nurtured, the concerns that we have as individuals, our religious outlook. There is no neutral ground on which to stand, no objective view of the text. Equally important, there is no single, proper, authoritative way to read the Bible. Rather, there are multiple ways of reading, and the interactions among them could challenge, correct, and expand our understanding of Scripture. In this ongoing process, our century, the twenty-first, must seek to read the Bible anew.

So we return to the point where we began: the "dramatic movement of the Bible." The Bible belongs above all to the community of faith! For Christians as well as Jews, the Bible

is the story of the people of God who celebrate its denouement in worship. In the Eucharist, Christians remember and
celebrate the Christ Event as the crucial event of the Bible and,
in their vision, of all history. At Passover, Jews remember and
celebrate the root experience of the Exodus. In both cases, the
worshipping community participates in a divine drama set in
motion by the God who is Creator of the cosmos and Ruler of
history—the continual unfolding in the present of "the story
of our lives."

Notes

Introducing the Bible Study

1. Paul Lehmann, *The Death of Jesus Christ: A Bible Study on What Led Christians to Study the Bible* (New York: United Student Christian Council, 1951).

2. Some interpreters use the term "redemptive history" or "salvation history" (German: *Heilsgeschichte*). See Will Herberg's illuminating essay "Biblical Faith as *Heilsgeschichte*" (cited in Suggestions for Further Reading). See also the postscript to this book, "Reading the Bible in the Twenty-First Century."

3. Four passages are selected for each study unit. If only one session is devoted to each unit, the leader will have to determine which passage should be the focus of discussion. Otherwise, the group may want to stay with a particular unit for more than one session.

4. This point is developed in my essay "The Contemporaneity of the Bible" (cited in Suggestions for Further Reading).

5. Amos Wilder, *The Language of the Gospel* (New York: Harper and Row, 1964), 64–65.

Prologue: In the Beginning

1. For further elucidation of Israel's creation belief in relation to that of ancient religions, see my *Creation versus Chaos* (cited in Suggestions for Further Reading), especially chapter 1, "Creation and History." See also my "Introduction: Mythopoeic and Theological Dimensions of Biblical Creation Faith" in *Creation in the Old Testament* (cited in Suggestions for Further Reading).

2. In some of my essays I have explored more fully the metaphorical character of biblical language: "Cosmic Dimensions

of the Biblical Creation Account," postscript to *Creation versus Chaos* (cited in Suggestions for Further Reading); "A Stylistic Study of the Priestly Creation Account," in *Canon and Authority* (ed. G. W. Coats and B. O. Long; Philadelphia: Fortress Press, 1977), 148–62; and my introduction to *The Books of the Bible*, "The Bible as Sacred Scripture" (ed. B. W. Anderson; New York: Charles Scribner's, 1989).

3. See "Creation and Worship," in my *Creation versus Chaos* (cited in Suggestions for Further Reading).

4. For a fuller discussion of these two accounts in the history of Israelite tradition, see the section, "The Primeval History," in chapter 5 of my *Understanding the Old Testament* (cited in Suggestions for Further Reading), and the section, "The Priestly Point of View," in chapter 13.

5. See "Creation and the Noachic Covenant," in my *Contours of Old Testament Theology*, chapter 11 (cited in Suggestions for Further Reading).

6. For discussion of environmental (ecological) issues connected with the "image of God," see my "Human Dominion over Nature," in *Biblical Studies in Contemporary Thought* (ed. Miriam Ward; Burlington, Vt.: Trinity College Biblical Institute, 1975; distributed by Greeno, Hadden); and my "Creation and Ecology," in *Creation in the Old Testament* (cited in Suggestions for Further Reading). For an excellent commentary, turn to Walter Brueggemann, *Genesis* (cited in Suggestions for Further Reading).

7. Herbert Butterfield, *Christianity and History* (New York: Charles Scribner's, 1950), 6–7. For further discussion of the relationship between creation and science, see the essays—including my own ("The Earth Is the Lord's")—in *Is God a Creationist? The Religious Case against Creation-Science* (ed. Roland M. Frye; New York: Charles Scribner's, 1983).

8. See the exquisite treatment of this story from a feminist point of view by Phyllis Trible in "A Love Story Gone Awry" (cited in Suggestions for Further Reading).

A Way into the Future

1. See the excellent discussion of Martin Luther King's use of biblical imagery by James H. Smylie in "On Jesus, Pharaohs, and the Chosen People: Martin Luther King as Biblical Interpreter and Humanist," *Interpretation* (1970): 74–91.

2. For a discussion of literary and historical problems, see the first two chapters in my *Understanding the Old Testament* (cited in Suggestions for Further Reading).

3. Some classic discussions of this subject are Martin Buber's *I and Thou* (New York: Charles Scribner's, 1937); his *Eclipse of God* (New York: Harper, 1952); and H. Richard Niebuhr's *The Meaning of Revelation* (New York: Macmillan, 1941).

4. In some modern translations, such as the New Revised Standard Version, the sacred name is translated "the Lord," following synagogue practice. The New Jerusalem Bible translates "Yahweh." For a clear and profound discussion of the giving of God's name, see Gerhard von Rad, *Moses* (World Christian Books; New York: Association Press, 1960), pp. 18–25. See also "The Name of God," chapter 6, in my *Contours of Old Testament Theology* (cited in Suggestions for Further Reading).

5. An admirable, nontechnical discussion of the Mosaic covenant in the light of ancient political treaties is found in Delbert Hillers, *Covenant: The History of a Biblical Idea* (cited in Suggestions for Further Reading).

The Discipline of Disaster

1. See "The Promises of Grace to David," chapter 23, in my *Contours of Old Testament Theology* (cited in Suggestions for Further Reading).

2. See further my discussion of prophecy in "The Shock of God's Future," chapter 2 of *The Eighth Century Prophets: Amos, Hosea, Isaiah, Micah* (cited in Suggestions for Further Reading).

3. For a fuller discussion of Jeremiah and his times, see chapter 12 in my *Understanding the Old Testament* (cited in Suggestions for Further Reading).

4. The covenant lawsuit is indicated by the Hebrew verb in verse 9 translated "contend." This literary genre is discussed by Delbert Hillers in *Covenant: The History of a Biblical Idea* (Baltimore: Johns Hopkins University Press, 1969), chapter 6. See also the discussion of Jeremiah in my *Contours of Old Testament Theology*, chapter 22, "Prophecy in the Mosaic Tradition," especially pp. 186–87.

5. The Isaiah passage also inspired Harry Emerson Fosdick's hard-hitting sermon, "God Talks to a Dictator," included in *Living under Tension: Sermons on Christianity Today* (New York: Harper, 1941), 172–81.

6. Herbert Butterfield, *Christianity and History* (New York: Charles Scribner's, 1950).

7. See my exposition of this passage, "The New Covenant and the Old," in *The Old Testament and Christian Faith* (New York: Herder and Herder, 1969; orig. publ. New York: Harper and Row, 1963).

The New Exodus

1. While "Israel" refers to the whole people of God, "the Jews" originally designated the residents of Judah, the Southern Kingdom—that is, Judeans—who were exiled from the land of Judah. "Samaritans," on the other hand, were the former citizens of Samaria, the Northern Kingdom, who previously had been exiled by the Assyrians.

2. For a discussion of the theology of social stability represented by the Davidic covenant, see my *Contours of Old Testament Theology*, Part II-C, "The Davidic Covenant."

3. For more on the motif of the New Exodus, see my "Exodus Typology in Second Isaiah," in *Israel's Prophetic Heritage* (cited in Suggestions for Further Reading).

4. Besides this chapter, there are three other Servant poems: Isa 42:1-4; 49:1-6; 50:4-9. The identity of the servant in Second Isaiah is a moot question. See my discussion in the section called "The Servant of YHWH," in chapter 14 of *Understanding the Old Testament* (cited in Suggestions for Further Reading).

The People of the Torah

1. For a discussion of these developments, see chapter 15 of my *Understanding the Old Testament* (cited in Suggestions for Further Reading).

2. See my *Out of the Depths* (cited in Suggestions for Further Reading), especially chapter 7.

3. Aage Bentzen, *Introduction to the Old Testament*, 4th ed. (Copenhagen: G. E. C. Gads Vorlag, 1958), 2:170.

4. For further discussion of the Book of Job, see especially Samuel Terrien, *Job, Poet of Existence*, and "The Book of Job" in chapter 17 of my *Understanding the Old Testament*. On the problem of undeserved suffering, see my *Contours of Old Testament Theology*, chapter 31, "The Justice of God," especially pp. 276–82 (all are cited in Suggestions for Further Reading).

Victory through Defeat

1. In T. S. Eliot, *Collected Poems, 1909–1962* (Harcourt, Brace, 1963), 199. Used by permission.

2. The Essene community of Qumran thought of itself as the eschatological community of the new covenant. More can be found out about this community by turning to, among other sources, James C. VanderKam, *The Dead Sea Scrolls Today* (Grand Rapids, Mich.: Eerdmans, 1994); and Geza Vermes, *The Complete Dead Sea Scrolls in English*, rev. ed. (New York: Penguin Classics, 2004).

3. Amos Wilder, *The Language of the Gospel*, 64–65 (cited in Suggestions for Further Reading).

The Church in the World

1. On this and related psalms, see my *Out of the Depths*, 3rd ed. (Louisville: Westminster John Knox, 2000), especially chapter 6.

2. Some scholars believe that Ephesians is "deutero-Pauline," that is, written by a disciple whose thinking was closely akin to Paul's. The words "at Ephesus" are lacking in Eph 1:1 in the best manuscripts, and the tone of the letter is quite general, without

reference to local conditions at Ephesus in Asia Minor (modern Turkey). Others hold that this is a general letter that Paul intended for reading in a number of churches in Asia Minor.

3. Martin Buber, *I and Thou* (New York: Charles Scribner's, 1937), 45.

Epilogue: In the End

1. The word "apocalyptic" comes from the Greek *apocalypse*, which means "revelation" to a seer. The best example of this type of literature in the Old Testament is the book of Daniel, likewise written in a time of persecution (about 165 BCE). For a discussion of Daniel, see the section, "The Kingdom That Is God's," in chapter 18 of my *Understanding the Old Testament* (cited in Suggestions for Further Reading).

2. The "sea" or "chaos" imagery is discussed at length in my *Creation versus Chaos* (Eugene, Ore.: Wipf and Stock, 2005), especially chapters 4 and 5.

3. The biblical hope for a future life is expressed not in the Greek doctrine of the immortality of the soul, which presupposes a deathless element imprisoned in the body, but in the apocalyptic category of resurrection of the person. For an interpretation of the words of the Apostles' Creed, "I believe in the resurrection of the body," see Reinhold Niebuhr, *Beyond Tragedy* (New York: Charles Scribner's, 1938).

4. For a discussion of the transformation of the body in apocalyptic vision, see chapter 34, "Life, Death, and Resurrection," in my *Contours of Old Testament Theology* (cited in Suggestions for Further Reading).

5. Oscar Cullmann, *Christ and Time* (Philadelphia: Westminster, 1950), 81–93. He observes: "That which has already happened offers the solid guarantee for that which will take place. The hope of the final victory is so much the more vivid because of the unshakably firm conviction that the battle that decides the victory has already taken place" (87).

6. The word *rapture* comes from the Latin *raptus* (Vulgate translation), which renders a Greek verb meaning to "seize,"

"snatch away," or "transport suddenly." The passage suggests to some that people will be seized by Christ and lifted beyond themselves.

7. See, for example, John Polkinghorne, *The Faith of a Physicist* (Augsburg Fortress Publishers, 1996). An Anglican priest as well as a scientist, Polkinghorne argues that the resurrection is a historical event—the only one of its kind, which marks a turning point in human and cosmic history.

Suggestions for Bible Study Leaders

1. Thomas Merton, *Opening the Bible*, 11 (cited in Suggestions for Further Reading).

2. See my *The Living Word of the Bible*, especially pp. 34–35 (cited in Suggestions for Further Reading).

Reading the Bible in the Twenty-First Century

1. The phrase "the dramatic movement of Scripture" comes from my presentation celebrating the sesquicentennial of Union Theological Seminary, April 9, 1987; see *Union Seminary Quarterly Review* 42 (1988): 38–41. Some thoughts in this postscript are also included in my preface to *Understanding the Old Testament*, 5th ed. (Upper Saddle River, N.J.: Pearson Prentice Hall, 2006).

2. Abraham Joshua Heschel, *God in Search of Man: A Philosophy of Judaism* (New York: Farrar, Straus, and Giroux, 1976), 254.

3. H. Richard Niebuhr, *The Meaning of Revelation* (New York: Macmillan, 1941), chapter 2.

4. Amos Wilder, *The Language of the Gospel* (New York: Harper and Row, 1964), 64–65.

Professor Bernhard W. Anderson speaks at Princeton Theological Seminary.

About the Author

BERNHARD W. ANDERSON

*Professor of Old Testament Theology Emeritus,
Princeton Theological Seminary*

Bernhard W. Anderson has devoted his career to the interpretation of the Bible through teaching, lecturing. and writing. He is perhaps best known for his widely-used textbook, *Understanding the Old Testament* (5th edition, 2006).

A graduate of the College of the Pacific (now the University of the Pacific) in Stockton, California (1936), Dr. Anderson received his divinity degree from the Pacific School of Religion in 1939 and was ordained as a minister of the United Methodist Church. As a minister, he served Methodist churches in various communities in the San Francisco bay area, including Sunnyvale and Millbrae.

With the encouragement of James Muilenburg, his teacher at the Pacific School of Religion, Dr. Anderson moved east to pursue graduate studies in the Old Testament field, receiving his Ph.D. from Yale University in 1945. He began his teaching career in 1946 at Colgate University in Hamilton, New York, and from there moved to teaching positions at the University of North Carolina (1948-50) and Colgate-Rochester Divinity School in Rochester, New York (1950-54).

In 1954 Dr. Anderson was invited to become Dean of the Theological School of Drew University in Madison, New Jersey. During his administration, he gathered and led a distinguished faculty that included, among others, Karlfried Froehlich, Robert Funk, Howard Kee, Gordon Harland, and Will Herberg. He also continued his teaching career as the Henry A. Buttz Professor of Biblical Theology.

While at Drew, Dr. Anderson developed a special interest in archaeology. In 1956 he joined with the late George Ernest Wright to launch the Drew-McCormick Archaeological Expedition for the purpose of excavating the site of the ancient biblical city of Shechem. In 1963-64 he served as Annual Professor of the American School of Oriental Research (now the Albright Biblical Institute) in Jerusalem, from which base he conducted archaeological field trips into Jordan, Lebanon, Syria, Iraq, Iran, and Egypt.

In 1968 Dr. Anderson became Professor of Old Testament Theology at Princeton Theological Seminary, a position he held until his retirement in 1983.

In retirement Dr. Anderson has continued to teach and lecture widely. From 1984 to 1996 he was Adjunct Professor of Old Testament Theology for one semester each year at the Boston University School of Theology. On leave from that position, he spent the 1985-86 academic year as Visiting Professor of Old Testament at Union Theological Seminary in New York City. He was Visiting Professor of Old Testament at Yale Divinity School in the spring semester of 1988, and Visiting Professor of Religion at Middlebury College, Vermont, in spring 1989. He has also led numerous bible study groups both in the United States and abroad.

Dr. Anderson has served as President of the Society of Biblical Literature (1980) and President of the American Theological Society (1985). In 1980 the Society of Biblical Literature presented him with the Julian Morgenstern Award "in recognition of his unusual success in sharing the results of biblical scholarship with a very wide audience." He has honorary degrees from the Pacific School of Religion (D.D., 1960), the University of the Pacific (S.T.D., 1961), and Colgate University (D.D. 1965).

Other Books by Bernhard W. Anderson

Understanding the Old Testament

Contours of Old Testament Theology

Out of the Depths: The Psalms Speak For Us Today

From Creation to New Creation: Old Testament Perspectives

*Creation versus Chaos: the Reinterpretation
of Mythical Symbolism in the Bible*

The Eighth Century Prophets: Amos, Hosea, Isaiah, Micah

Creation Theology as a Basis for Global Witness

Lent

The Living Word of the Bible

Rediscovering the Bible

Editor/Contributor

Creation in the Old Testament

The Books of the Bible

Will Herberg, *Faith Enacted as History:
Essays in Biblical Theology*

Israel's Prophetic Heritage: Essays in Honor of James Muilenburg

*The Old Testament and Christian Faith:
A Theological Discussion*

Translator

Martin Noth, *A History of Pentateuchal Traditions*

Printed in the USA
CPSIA information can be obtained
at www.ICGtesting.com
JSHW082014220823
47026JS00004B/19